SAIL WITH JIM

SAIL WITH JIM

The Dream

JAMES G WHITELAW

CONTENTS

1 THE FIRST 50 YEARS — 3

1. The First Sail — 4
2. Cementing the Future — 12
3. Background — 18

2 LADY TOO — 21

4. Searching for the Boat — 22
5. Bringing her Home — 25
6. Summer 2009 — 32
7. Summer 2010 — 34
8. Summer 2011 — 36
9. April 2012 Banff to Inverness — 45
10. Through the Caledonian Canal — 53
11. Corpach to Barcaldine, Loch Creran — 58

| 12 | Barcaldine to Loch Liurboist, Isle of Lewis | 60 |

3
PUNTO DI SVOLTA — 73

13	The educated search	74
14	The purchase and planning	77
15	Felixstowe to Scarborough	84
16	Scarborough to Peterhead	93
17	Winter's work	97

4
A LOOK AHEAD TO SAIL WITH JIM 2013 — 101

5
UPDATE 2021 — 103

Introduction

Sail with Jim – The Dream
by James G Whitelaw
Copyright James G Whitelaw 2021

I dedicate this book to Albert Robertson and my Uncle Jim, who first introduced me to sailing.

As a young lad of only ten years old, Jim Whitelaw is taken sailing with a friend of the family. Jim is totally enthralled and from that day forward Jim decides that one day he will buy his own yacht. It is forty years later before Jim eventually keeps his promise to himself and this book reflects the story and steep learning curve during Jim's forty-year journey. Jim buys his first boat without too much knowledge and makes many mistakes and gets into quite a few scrapes. This book follows Jim's dream and nightmares.

-

PART 1

The First 50 years

CHAPTER 1

The First Sail

The first sail

I am not sure how old I was. Certainly it was a very long time ago from my now 61 years old. It must have been around 50 years ago, probably around 1970 or thereabouts.

Early on a fine summer's Saturday morning, Albert Robertson, a close family friend, and also the highly esteemed and very well respected local dentist arrived to pick up my cousin Robert and myself to go sailing on his small yacht which he kept in Gamrie harbour. We were going to sail the yacht from Gamrie up to Banff.

Gamrie is the local name for a village in the north-east of Scotland which has the real name of Gardenstown. The village was founded by the local superior, Alexander Garden of Troup in 1720, and is today regarded as one of the major influences in the UK fishing industry.

Albert owned a holiday cottage in the neighbouring, but smaller village of Crovie, and berthed his yacht in Gamrie harbour during the summer. I don't know which model of yacht the "Kittiwake" was, but I do remember it very clearly and estimate it at around 17 feet long. It had a drop keel and an outboard engine if I remember correctly, but things are starting to get a little fuzzy now. I suspect it was a Leisure 17 or similar type of yacht.

It was all white with a small porthole window forward in the cabin at either side. Whoever had painted on the name, you didn't get computer generated vinyl graphics in those days, had made a very good job of it, and on each side, up forward on the hull, not only was the name prominent, but it was proceeded with a very good picture of a kittiwake.

It was like going on holiday. I was so excited. I had been around boats all my life, my dad and my entire mother's family being fishermen, but this was different. This was a yacht.

Maybe these ocean going sailors would laugh at me, but if a boat had sails, to me it was, and still is, a yacht, regardless of size, and yachts were exciting in a way which fishing boats were not. There was something about going through the sea without any engine noise, peaceful and quiet, free and gliding like a bird soaring on the thermals.

This first trip kindled an interest in me which was never to be suppressed, and although it was to be another 40 years before I bought my first yacht, the deal was sealed on that day.

I am not sure how long Albert had owned the yacht, but he certainly seemed to know what he was doing and imparted some of that knowledge to our young heads, as best as he could. Albert would sit at the helm and instruct Robert and myself in handling the sails and ropes.

The "Kittiwake" was a light responsive boat which sailed well even in light winds. Around our coastline, there were thousands of Kittiwakes, a small seabird, like a miniature seagull, but cute and without the harsh predator look of the bigger bird. Albert pointed these out to us and explained where the yacht's name came from. There were literally thousands of birds which nested on the cliffs of nearby Troup head, which has since been declared a bird sanctuary.

I am sure we had some sandwiches and drinks packed somewhere in a little bag, as we were always hungry at that age, but to tell you the truth.

My memories don't extend to trivial little items like that, but to the more important things.

We travelled down to Gamrie in Albert's Citroen. In those days there weren't many foreign cars on the road, not like today, so the car was a bit of a mystery too. I don't think I had experienced much beyond Ford, British Leyland and Roots cars. For young people who don't remember, Roots was the name which Chrysler had at that point. I won't even try to explain British Leyland; you will have to Google it. It really is a different world 50 years down the road.

Arriving in Gamrie, 6-7 miles from our home in Macduff, we wound down the brae in a small village which was completely different from our home a few miles away. In fact it was so different; it could have been in a foreign country. The culture was different, life's pace was a little slower, and they even seemed to speak a different language.

Albert seemed to understand the language though, and know the locals, so perhaps we would survive. Little did I know that only about 10 years later, I would marry a young girl from this "foreign" village, and less than 20 years later, would move to stay here with my family.

Driving down the steep brae, you could see the harbour long before you reached it. It kept disappearing and re-appearing as we wound our way round the ever descending hairpin bends on "Gamrie Brae". If you are reading this book, and have never been to Gamrie, then I have to say, you have missed out on one of the most beautiful spots in Scotland. Make a plan to visit, but best do it in the summer, as it can be a very remote and bleak place in the winter, like many of Scotland's treasures.

We eventually parked up on the pier at Gamrie, and the harbour was full of little fishing boats. Most of them were small creel boats (Lobster pot boats for the English), but right there, out in the middle of the harbour was the Kittiwake. In fact, many of the boats were out in the middle of the harbour. I wondered how the owners got to them, and how we would get out to the Kittiwake.

We stood on the pier and looked out to the Kittiwake and I hoped that I didn't have to swim out to it. We did swim a lot in sea in those days, and didn't mind the cold, but I didn't have a towel with me today to dry myself, and I had no "dookers" (Swimming trunks).

Albert took off to the south pier and we toddled behind. He located a rope on the pier which he loosed out quite a bit. Back to the East pier where another rope was located and pulled in, bringing the Kittiwake right alongside a ladder so we could board her.

I was in my element. For the first time in my life, I was on-board a yacht. Young though I was, I would begin to learn a little about how a sailing boat worked, what all the ropes were for, but right now it was all a mystery.

I am sure Albert must have had some preparation to do before we were ready. There was a small red tank with fuel we had taken down with us in the car, and down the ladder. I guess that had to go somewhere. To be honest, I don't remember a whole lot. I just remember untying the Kittiwake and leaving the ropes attached to a buoy and the ladder to be retrieved later when we returned with the boat.

Actually, we never returned to the buoy. Although we did make this westward journey a number of times, we always left the boat in Banff, so I guess someone else must have sailed the boat back with him, or maybe he did it single handed, like I tend to do on most of my trips.

With the outboard engine running, we motored out of Gamrie harbour into the shelter of the "Muckle rock", which guarded the harbour entrance. We rounded the rock, and once out into "Gamrie Bay"; we got the sails up and shut off the engine. We began to move along by sail power only. I don't have a date, a time, or even a year, but this was the exact time when my love of yachts was born.

We sailed out of Gamrie Bay and out past Mhor head, one of the two mighty pillars which dominate and guard Gamrie Bay. In Gamrie bay, there is a strip, just a few miles wide, which is made up of crumbling red sandstone. This strip runs about twenty miles inland past Turriff, and you can tell where it is, as you can see the old houses made out of the red stone. At Gamrie bay, at the western side, you have Mhor Head, a craggy outcrop which separates Gamrie from Greensides, a long sweeping rocky beach. On the eastern side, you have the massive granite headland of Troup Head, which is one of the most important colonies of sea birds in the north of Scotland.

High up on Mhor there is an ancient church, "The Church of St John the Evangelist", which was built to commemorate a victory over the Vikings at the point of Mhor in the year 1004AD. The "Battle of the Bloody Pits" was a resounding victory against a foe that were pretty formidable, and the skulls of three of the Danish chieftains could be seen in an alcove in the church walls until about 1970, when the skulls were stolen. They were subsequently recovered but are now kept in Banff museum for safe keeping.

It is amazing how different places look from the sea, as opposed from the land. If you are planning a visit to Gamrie, then do try to get a trip out to sea to view the village from there. One of the local creel boats will oblige, and you could even have the opportunity to help them pull their creels. I remember my days as a fisherman and when you looked along the coastline at night, from the sea, Gamrie looked bigger than some places ten times its size, simply because it was built on a hill.

The house I have in Gamrie now is at the top of the village. It is only about ¼ mile from the harbour, but it is up at 140m, or around 450 feet in "old money". From the sea, you get an absolute spectacular view of Gamrie, the entire village. None of it is hidden. Each part is higher up than the street below, so you see it all. At night, from the sea, it looks like a city, even though there are only around 200 homes there.

I am sure Albert had sailed this route a number of times before, as he was able to keep us fairly close into land and keep the trip interesting for us. Round Mhor head, heading west, you come into "Greensides", which is a long sweeping bay, full of rocks with no possible landing place for anything other than a very knowledgeable local with a small boat. In days long ago, there was some salmon fishery carried out here and there are the remains of a salmon bothy at the far western side of the cove. There is also a very rough, steep track where some poor horse would have had to pull up a cart loaded with fish and equipment, and even their boats. The cliffs which surround Greensides are all around five hundred feet high, and any time I have been down there, I was always breathing very hard before I got back up to the top. For this very reason, it is very much an unspoilt beach.

There are a series of bays like this all along the coast, each one different and interesting, and all the way to Macduff, including one which opens up into a series of gorges containing all the water which makes its way down to the sea from the area behind all these majestic cliffs. These are known as the "burns of Cullen" locally. The furthest east we had ventured as kids was the "Salmon Howe", but our mothers didn't know that. That was the sort of place you hadn't been told so, but you just knew, you weren't allowed to go there. It was a desolate deserted cove where, if anything were to happen to you, then you could lie there a long time before you would be discovered. It was east beyond Tarlair, up over the golf course and down the other side.

We sailed past the "Salmon Howe" and into the bay at Tarlair. Now we really were into home territory. We spent most of our free time in the summer at Tarlair outdoor swimming pool, one of the finest in the country, in those days. I remember summer days with Tarlair absolutely packed with thousands of people, pipe bands playing, galas, paddle boats..........those were the days. We would spend all our free time in the summer there, and even after school went back, we would rush home from school at four o clock and be changed, a quick bite to eat and off across the golf course and climbing down the cliffs to Tarlair in as short a time as possible.

The cold never seemed to bother us much in these days, and I begin to wonder about the kids today, and even about ourselves. Is it the introduction of central heating which has made us softer? I don't really know, but right through until the pool closed at the end of September, we would be there until they shut the gates at 8:30pm every night. Our mothers never had to wonder where we were in those days.

Just off the big pool at Tarlair, there is rock, right in the middle of the small protective bay. Albert expertly took us right into the bay, inside the rock, even to 20- 30 feet from the poolside. All the Saturday bathers look at us. Nobody had ever seen a boat come in there before. Robert and I had to stand in the bow and watch out for any rocks or boulders and shout back to Albert at the helm, so that he could take evasive action.

So we negotiated our way around the rock and back out to sea, in full view of envious bathers, some of which were our friends. I was on top of the world, so proud. Every one of those young boys eyes were glued to us as we sailed in so close to them, and then sailed off again. It must have been high tide, as I have seen that whole area dry with very dangerous looking rocks many of other times.

From there we continued our way past Berryden quarry, the "Black cove" and The Black Cove was another of these places you weren't allowed to go. These were the days before environmental awareness, and this was where the town dust cart deposited its load when it was full, straight into the sea.

It really makes you wonder. We have cleaned up our act so much these past forty years, and all of a sudden there are no fish in the sea, which had thrived there for thousands of years. Could it be that we are not as smart as we think we are, and we are actually interfering with nature and changing the order of things which have gone on for centuries?

Between the Black cove and the back of the harbour at Macduff there was a rocky beach, all of which we knew intimately, having scrambled over the rocks many times, fallen in, tumbled and gained many scratches, bruises, bumps and cuts, none of which I remember or did me any harm. Well, there was the one time we got cut off by the tide. I managed to jump across and only got my legs wet, but Robert hesitated a little too long, and in the end had to strip off, throw across his clothes and swim. He was just getting dressed again when our mothers appeared on the scene searching for us. It was well past our bed time, dark and they were pretty agitated. Hey, it was all good fun, part of life's learning curve, and in the end, we are still alive, aren't we? Mothers worry too much. So do wives!!!

Continuing our sail, we had to sail out past the "Collie rocks", which are a pretty dangerous set of rocks just off Macduff, mostly submerged just out of sight unless it is a real low tide, then out across Banff bay before taking down our sails and motoring into Banff harbour and tying the Kittiwake up. Forty years later, I still remember this day, the day which introduced me to my expensive hobby. Albert, if you are reading this, Pearl (my wife) says you have a lot to answer for.

Cementing the future

CHAPTER 2

Cementing the Future

We had a number of Saturday morning sails on the Kittiwake, each one as exciting as the first, each one reinforcing the thought, "One day, I am going to own my own yacht".

Unfortunately, we all get to that age where we find ourselves in a "Saturday job". For me it was more of a case of a summer job, and since the summer was sailing time, I guess the two just didn't fit together. All summer, for around four to five years, I used to go down and work with my uncle, "Jimmy Joiner".

Joiner was his last name, but in fact, he was a marine engineer, working on the many commercial fishing boats in Macduff and Whitehills harbour and often further afield. In the summertime, they were always very busy, as boats had scheduled regular maintenance for the period when the boat was tied up to allow the crew to go on the summer holidays.

I would assist them in stripping down and overhauling the old 6 cylinder Gardiner engines and even older 3 cylinder kelvin engines, usually being assigned the mundane task of cleaning up the cylinder heads, ready for refitting. I would work eight till five, Monday to Friday, back for five-thirty to eight-thirty on Monday, Tuesday and Thursday nights, and also eight till twelve on Saturday mornings.

I could probably fill another book with stories from this period in my life. Stories like the time I fell into the harbour in Whitehills, toolbox and all. Or how about the time I dropped the big 2 metre long steel governor pushrod on Andre's head. Oh He was angry, and I didn't run fast enough. These stories are for another time.

These were long working weeks for a young kid and during this time, the carefree reminders of sailing on the wind slipped from my mind.

I am not sure how many years later, years can seem like centuries when you are a kid, so it may well have been only one year, or could have been 3 or 4. One day, I came home from school, climbing the "Meter Hill", the local name for the top part of Skene Street, Macduff, where we stayed, and here, out in front of my Uncle Jim's house, 2 doors up from us, was a yacht on a cradle.

She was a beauty. I could see right away, she was not the same as the Kittiwake. She didn't have a drop keel. She had a massive fin keel, and in her cradle, she towered over me. She was a big boat. She must have been 26-28 feet, but looked massive to me at that age.

I don't remember her ever having a name, and I am not sure that my uncle Jim owned her very long, maybe even just one season or two. I do, however, remember going sailing a few times in her, mostly at nights, after school. This would have been just a little sailing around the bay, but again, to me, very exciting.

One particular sailing trip stuck in my mind, and taught me a lot about how these boats worked. We were coming back into Macduff harbour. My Uncle Jim berthed the boat on the long pier, just ahead of the Lifeboat berth, which was the first spot you came to when you entered through between the Long pier and the Duff Street jetty.

I guess the wind was favourable, and my uncle Jim decided that we would be able to come into the harbour under sail. My cousin Robert and I were each assigned a head sail rope for tacking, and after some practice all the way in, we had it down to a fine art.

As we entered the harbour channel, and especially as we came between the long pier and the West pier, there really wasn't much room for tacking, but I remember my uncle Jim, standing at the tiller, us waiting for his command. The boat would almost be touching the pier at one side before he swung the tiller and shouted out "NOW". One of us paid out while the other hauled in as fast as any professional race crew.

That was a very exciting entrance to the harbour, and I would turn over in my head these manoeuvres, coming to an understanding of how a sailing vessel worked. We were able to take the boat right into the harbour and tie it up without the need for an engine. This was invaluable training for me, as I would have to do this later in life a number of times, through necessity.

Through my teenager years, many other things took up possession of my mind, as they do, and sailing faded a little. The fascination, however, would never completely go away, and there was always a thought in my mind, "One day, I am going to own my own yacht".

Years later, after I was married, I think, we were up in Aviemore, and I spied the sailing dinghies for hire on Loch Morlich. There was a fresh breeze coming down the loch, but I talked my wife, Pearl into it anyway, and hired a sailing dinghy for a couple of hours.

These were very light boats, not like what I had sailed in before, but I knew the principles of how they worked was just the same, and knew how to make them go. Once I got it out there, right up to the line of buoys which the owner said I wasn't allowed to go past, I got her onto a broad reach and she was flying. Of course, we had to sit right up on the windward rail, as the dinghy was keeled over to the limit.

It only took minutes before Pearl was screaming and had to be rescued by the owner in his rib and taken ashore. She probably saw her whole life flash before her eyes, and was absolutely terrified. To me, that was what sailing boats were meant to do. It was great, and for the first time in my life, I was at the helm, flying along on the wind.

I guess you could say that Pearl was never going to encourage me to get a yacht. She had had quite enough on Loch Morlich to do her a lifetime. She was, later in life, to say to me, "I will be quite happy to go in a yacht with you, if you buy one which doesn't tip over". Tall order.

The next time I was sailing was probably twenty to twenty-five years later. It was the year 2000, and we had three days down in the Florida Keys, before going up to Orlando. Behind our hotel, there was a guy hiring Hobbie Kat catamarans. I hired the small vessel, I am not sure you could even call them a boat, for the entire day. There was a big inlet, probably around two miles across in both directions. My only restriction was I was not allowed out to the open sea.

I sailed around that inlet the whole day. Sometimes the kids would come with me, other times on my own. I did use sun cream, but you wouldn't have thought it. That night I had to go into a cold bath to try and cool my skin down. Again, though, I had a most enjoyable day, a memorable day, which stirred up the long pent up yearning inside me.

After the time in the Florida Keys, there was a definite reawakening of my interest in sailing. Many would be the time I would look out to the bay and see a sailing boat being carried along on the wind and wish I was there. I would also take time to stop and look at yachts lying in various marinas. There were some great examples on the Clyde, when we were visiting Pearl's auntie Rosaleen in Greenock.

Gamrie harbour was always full of small creel boats, but they just didn't interest me, in fact, the smell was a real turn off. For lots of guys, there dream was to have a small creel boat and to shoot a few lobster pots. I am afraid that held no interest for me, much to my Father-in-law's regret.

My father-in-law loved his creel boat, and after retiring from the fishing, due to a heart attack, he had another twenty five years in which he enjoyed his boat. He used to look half dead in the wintertime, but when summer came, he would take on a new lease of life, and the boat was dully painted, launched and the creels, which he had painstakingly repaired over the winter, were brought out.

He loved his boat so much that often he would go out on it every day in the summer, even though some days he did not feel all that well. In the past few years though, his summers were becoming shorter as life started to catch up with him. At the end, he was found round in Greensides, a creel on his knees, having suffered a massive heart attack while out on the boat. It was hard for the family, but for him, it was his life, and the way he always said he wanted to go.

I did mute the idea of a boat with a few of the harbour committee in Gamrie, and got no encouragement at all, including from my own father-in-law. They just didn't want yachts in their harbour, only creel boats. For the older guys who had grown up in the really tough years, they just could not understand why anyone would want a boat from which you could not earn some money. It was non-productive and that just did not compute with them.

Now and then there were yachts in the harbour. The Laird had one there for a while, but then they could hardly deny the Laird a berth. There was also an old beat up yacht which Glen had in the harbour, which actually sank. I think this just reinforced the idea they did not want yachts in the harbour. I think the turning point for me was when my neighbour Iain got a yacht.

Iain already had moorings in the harbour, and he simply went and bought a yacht and put it onto the moorings. The old guys in the harbour probably weren't really happy, but he got away with it, and the door was opened. That was probably the point when I made up my mind to start a serious search for a yacht. It probably tied in with the realisation that I wasn't getting any younger, and if I were to do this, then I realistically couldn't afford to wait much longer.

Around ten years previously, I had had a little spare cash and had toyed with the idea of buying a yacht. We had also visited Florida that year and I really liked Florida. It was either a yacht or a villa in Florida. Pearl didn't want either of them, but I guess the villa in Florida may have been the lesser of the two evils and she relented. The yacht was pushed back.

This time, 2007, there was to be no pushing back. I was not getting any younger. This had always been a dream, and I could not allow the idea that I would look back in twenty years' time, having missed the opportunity, and fading into old age with this regret hanging over me. I was finally going to get my own boat.

CHAPTER 3

Background

Background

As I write the next few chapters, there is absolutely no doubt that you are going to hear some strange tails, and observe some strange behaviour from me. I think, before we go there, it will help set the scene, if I give you some background to help you understand my thinking, sort of like trying to help you understand why I have done some of the crazy things I have done.

When I was 17, I went to the fishing to work. I can't ever say that I really liked it, but it was a job and it was really good money for a young lad. For seven years, I went to sea with my Uncle John on the Dioscuri and later on the Auriga. The "Swackies" were noted throughout the North East of Scotland for pushing it to the limit. They would go out to sea when other boats were tied up for bad weather. They would be the last boats to come back in when the weather deteriorated.

Some would say that they had no respect for the weather, but I would have to disagree. My Uncle John took the weather very seriously and never missed a shipping forecast. There was a healthy respect for the sea, but not a fear of it. He knew how far he could push it and get away with it.

He either taught me that same response to the sea or it has been passed on to me in my genes. I have a healthy respect for the sea, and have seen what it can do many times. One notable occasion was when we watched our sister ship, the "Mizpah" go down in a force 12 in November 1979. Fortunately, this time, there was no loss of life, but as fishermen, we all knew boats and men which had simply disappeared.

Like my uncle, I respect the sea, but there is a part of me which likes to push it to the limit, and I probably do not have the same fear of the sea as some other sailors, many of which have no sea-faring background at all. Many a time in my life, I have been absolutely soaked to the skin, and to me, that is simply part of going to sea. As long as I have a dry change of clothes to change into, it is no great problem.

I am also impulsive and impatient. This in itself is going to explain a whole lot later on. If I make up my mind to do something, then I just want to get on and do it. I will speed up and gloss over preparations to get it done faster. If I decide I am sailing somewhere, then my goal is to get there as fast as possible, no leisurely cruising, sailing only a few hours every day. You can cover a lot of ground when you sail overnight.

I don't like waste. I like to get the things I want in the most efficient way, and really don't like to buy anything I will rarely use. I am, however, willing to pay more for an item which will cover more than one purpose. I am often reluctant to replace items which still have a little use left in them. I like to get good use out of every item I pay for.

If I get a "bee in my bonnet", I can suffer from tunnel vision. Sometimes I am so focussed on something, that I do not properly examine other peripheral issues.

Finally, and perhaps the most important item, I am an eternal optimist. Sometimes this is a good thing, but at other times, which I have found out to my cost, it is not very good when you just cannot see the potential downside. If you cannot envision problems, then it is difficult to properly prepare for them.

I hope that this gives you a little insight into the mind of the author and that you can subsequently figure out why I did so many crazy things as you read through the book. I'm still here, so obviously I didn't push it too far, but I would have to say, I have changed my outlook some as a result of some of the mishaps and scrapes I got into. Maybe also as I get older, I like my comforts better and I am not quite so fit and able as I used to be when I was young and lithe.

Yes, those of you know me now; I was once young and fit. When I got married, I was strong as an ox and only ten and a half stone. This overweight, underpowered and unfit man which you all know is all Pearl's fault, or so I like to tease her. Married life has done this to me.

PART 2

Lady Too

Part Two – Lady Too

CHAPTER 4

Searching for the Boat

Searching for the boat

Summer 2007 saw me start to buy sailing magazines, searching through the "For sale" adverts and also to look longingly around marinas, paying particular attention to yachts for sale. I visited all the small harbours up and down our coast, not only looking at boats for sale, but also sizing up many of the different types of yachts available, and trying to figure out which type would be best for me.

I formulated some idea in my head of what I wanted. Firstly, a bilge, or twin keel boat would be necessary if I wanted to keep it in Gamrie harbour, as the berths all dry out at low tide. Secondly, it needed to be of a size which I could easily manage single handed, preferably around 22-28 feet long. Thirdly, it needed to have accommodation, as I wanted to sail a little further afield at times and stay on it overnight.

After looking at many different types of boats, I was very taken with the "Hunter Horizon", in particular, the 23 and 26 feet versions. I felt the 21 foot version was a little too small, and the 26 had everything I needed, so what would be the point of going any bigger. There was a nice 23 foot Horizon for sale in Findochty, the "Bramble", and I looked at it a number of times in the passing. The price the owner was asking, I felt, was a little high, so I did not take it any further.

A few years later, in a brief conversation with the owner's wife, she told me that I had almost bought their last yacht. This showed me two strange things. Firstly, I must have contacted them. I hadn't remembered that, as I had looked at so many yachts. Also I noted the term "our yacht". I just somehow couldn't imagine those words escaping from Pearl's lips. Any boat I did buy would most definitely be "his boat".

In the summer of 2008, I located a 26 foot Horizon down in Southampton and gave this very serious consideration. At £12k, it would be a large expenditure, similar to buying a car, and so I pondered over it for a while. Unfortunately, as I pondered, the biggest recession since 1929 was hitting the world, and my business was certainly not immune to it. I could see that cash was going to get tight, and decided that it would not be prudent to spend this amount of cash at the moment.

My son, Andrew, also decided that he would take an interest in sailing, and intimated that he would look with me and that we would "go halves" when we finally bought a boat. He was looking through eBay and spied a 20 feet Vivacity which was in Inverness. The advert stated that she was fully kitted out and ready to go sailing, and although she was almost 40 years old, we thought that this may be worth considering further.

The seller was asking £2,500 for the boat, and it certainly wasn't going to break the bank. We also considered that it might be good to start with a cheaper boat, learn the ropes, make any mistakes and try it out, before getting a bigger and better boat. In the end, we decided to put in a cheeky offer of £2,000 and it was accepted, to our surprise.

I guess we put the offer in, not really expecting it to be taken seriously, and it was a surprise to us too that we suddenly found ourselves the owner of a boat, not really the type which we wanted, but it was ours now, and we had to go with it. We hadn't even viewed the boat, which was lying at Muirtown marina in Inverness. So, we found ourselves on the train to Inverness, and once again, imposing on "Auntie Rosleen and Uncle Donald" for an overnight stay before sailing her home the next day.

CHAPTER 5

Bringing her Home

Bringing her home

Pearl, my wife, dropped Andrew and me off at Keith station where we boarded a train to Inverness. Donald and Rosaleen met us at Inverness station and took us down to Muirtown to view the boat.

At this point, I think I need to say that you are going to read a fair bit about Donald and Rosaleen. Rosaleen is a sister of my wife's father, and to be honest, everyone should have an "Auntie Rosaleen". I would never manage to pay her back for all her hospitality over the years, and for all the times I have simply turned up on her doorstep. You will see what I mean later.

Lady Too lay in Muirtown marina, and was better than many of the clapped out vessels which lay there, but at only £2k, we weren't expecting too much, and we weren't disappointed. Everything was there which you needed to sail her, but it was a basic package. Of course, being our first purchase, we probably didn't quite know what to look for, so it was pretty much going to be a case of buy it, then see how it went.

She had a trailer, but we had already decided that we would rather sail her home and collect the trailer at a later date. The trailer, like the rest of the package, was a little dilapidated and I am not sure it would have been wise to take her on an 80 mile journey with a weight of over one ton.

We had a good look around the boat, made some notes of things which we needed, then headed back to Auntie Rosaleen's for the night. We took a trip to the shops for a few things which we might need and planned to get down to the boat fairly early in the morning, so we could get down the Muirtown staircase (series of locks) and out into the sea to catch the tide at 10:30am.

The next morning, the 11th September 2008, we arrived at Muirtown around 9:00am and immediately started to descend the series of locks. This canal is a monument to Thomas Telford who was the architect in charge of building the canal. It really was a huge undertaking in those days when there was no mechanical help, and to think that it is still standing today, almost two hundred years later is testament to the quality of the work, which cost less than one million pounds to complete the full 62 miles long waterway.

There are 4 locks in the staircase at Muirtown and then the swing bridge at the bottom. This takes you into Muirtown basin which is a large harbour and berthing facility. At the sea end of the basin, there is another swing bridge for the railway and another set of locks.

The trains take priority over boats, and we had to wait for a couple of trains to pass before we could have the bridge swung open and pass through into the next set of locks. After passing through the locks, there are two piers which extend well into the Beauly Firth, with the sea locks at the end. I believe these were particularly difficult to build when the canal was constructed as there were high silt build up all along this stretch of coast, which necessitated the need for these two long piers to go well out into the firth. The sea locks are the main administrative points for the canal, and the lock keeper wanted to see our licence. I had assumed that as the boat was in the canal, we would be OK to take it out, but a sixty pound fee later, I discovered that I had assumed wrongly, and it was quite an expensive two hour journey down to the sea.

We finally made it into the open sea around midday, and motored out into the middle of the firth before putting up the sails. We hadn't even looked at the sails the previous day, and this was our first opportunity to assess them. I guess you would say that was a little silly, but then we weren't quite sure what we were looking for and we were in a bit of a hurry. The forward genoa looked to be in pretty good shape, but the main sail looked like it could have been part of the original kit for the boat and had certainly seen better days.

There wasn't a whole lot of wind and we had up all our sail and were moving quite slowly down the firth. We passed under the Kessock Bridge and were fairly happy with our purchase and enjoying the pleasant sail down the firth. We were so busy looking at different things on the boat, discussing, planning and debating what repairs and improvements were needed, that we didn't see the squall approaching from behind us until it hit us, and the boat suddenly broached, and hauled her head to the wind.

We both got a bit of a scare, but Andrew, especially, almost dirtied his pants. I have never asked Andrew, but I am sure he would tell me that this was the moment he decided that maybe sailing wasn't for him. Once we composed ourselves, we looked up at the sails and the mainsail was split right along one of the joins in the canvas. We had no alternative but to take the sail down and continue with just the genoa. The genoa was a big sail, and as the wind was on the quarter, she sailed pretty good with just the genoa up.

We went further down the firth and dropped the anchor off Ardersier so that we could assess the situation. Andrew was clearly shaken and I just could not talk him into putting the sail back up. He was used to small boats, as he had owned one since he was about ten years old, and had also gone to sea with his Granddad, pulling lobster pots and fishing for mackerel, but this was a different kettle of fish altogether, and he didn't like it.

Andrew suggested that the best option was to motor round to Nairn, leave the boat there and come back for it another day. I really wasn't keen on leaving the boat in Nairn, and I countered that I drop him off in Nairn and take the boat home myself. This he shook his head at and reluctantly agreed to, just the same as I reluctantly agreed to motor round to Nairn instead of using the sails.

We motored through the narrows between Fort George and Channonry point, where a strong tide runs, and extra care and attention is required to the times of the tides. This is the reason we wanted to exit the canal at 10:30am so that we could catch the ebb tide for going through these narrows. We still had two hours of tide, so had no problems going through the narrows, then taking the inside shallow channel around the sandbank which lies outside the firth.

Taking the south channel means keeping pretty close to the land and it was very interesting to see a new perspective of this area which I had not seen before. It was especially interesting to view Fort George and to realise how vitally important this strong fort had been in days when a naval presence was essential to the defence of the land. In the days when the main mode of transport was by sea, it was obvious how important and dominant a position like this would have been.

Further round there was the more recent development of Ardersier yard where they built many of the early North Sea platforms, but now sadly lying disused. There has been much talk over the years of reviving the yard, turning it into a marina and such like things, but so far, the yard is still lying dilapidated and unused, which is a shame for such a great deep water facility. Potential developers may have an eye on the conversion to a marina of a similar facility at Portavadie, on the Clyde, which has been less than successful, in my mind, due to its remote location.

From Channonry point to Nairn, indeed, all the way to Burghead, there are miles of sandy beaches which would be worth a fortune to the local economy if we could only get the weather which the Mediterranean enjoys. There wasn't much to see as we motored along these lovely, but empty beaches, the eight or nine miles to Nairn, but again it was very interesting to see a perspective on a an area I had seen plenty of, but which now look so different..

I went in as far as the nearest ladder at Nairn and Andrew happily scrambled up onto the pier, delighted to be back on dry land. I cast off and turned her head back to sea without any delay. Andrew spoke to a few older guys on the pier, and they were shaking their heads that I was going back out in this terrible weather. They obviously hadn't gone to sea with the "Swackies", and in my mind in wasn't all that bad a day. I would have estimated it as a force four or five, and I was to take this little boat out in worse, during my ownership of her.

As I was leaving the pier, the engine cut out, and rather than fiddle around with it, I simply rolled out the genoa and was off again. According to the log, I was making around five knots, which was fairly good progress. I kept fairly close to the land again, and noted the sandbanks which lay all along this coast. It was interesting to see the different objects which I had studied on the chart and in the pilot book, possible anchorages, inlets, sandbanks to avoid and landmarks. Things always look so different in reality to what you imagine them, having noted them on a chart.

Once I passed the entrance to Findhorn Bay, there is a long sweeping sandy beach all the way to Burghead, so I set off to cut across this bay, rather than hug the land, which would save me an hour on my journey. Being on my own, I realised that I could not keep going all night, and so began to contemplate where I would take a rest. I knew that Burghead was a fairly decent harbour, but the next suitable place where I could enter at any tide would be Lossiemouth. I decided that I would go into Burghead and take a sleep, before continuing the next day. With a little more experience under my belt, I would have kept going, but I had yet to learn a few important lessons of sailing.

I went into Burghead around 7:00pm, had something to eat and went to bed about 8:00pm. I awoke at 1:00am and got underway again. I sailed out of Burghead and cleared the rocks round the corner and sailed under the cliffs along to Hopeman. At around 3:00am, off of Hopeman, unfortunately, the wind died and I was making very little headway, and so I reluctantly started the engine to help me out.

This is when I began to consider the petrol we had already used when motoring round to Nairn, when we could have been sailing. I knew that I would need more petrol, but the question was where would I get it? I could go into Lossiemouth, but there would be nowhere open at 4:00am, and I wasn't quite sure where the petrol station was in Lossiemouth. I knew there was a petrol station right at the harbour in Buckie, so decided that I would be best to head for Buckie, rather than wait around for 4 hours in Lossiemouth.

I was midway between Lossiemouth and Buckie when the engine spluttered and died from lack of fuel, so it was back to the sails, and with very little wind, I finally struggled into Buckie at 1:00pm. It is always difficult coming into a harbour under sail power only, although I have done it a number of times. It is OK until you enter into the harbour, then you generally lose any little wind there is, due to the height of the piers.

I managed to get alongside the first pier end where there were a number of people ready to take a rope and help me out. The harbourmaster was there and was none too pleased at me as I didn't have a VHF radio, and he had been trying to contact me. He urged me to go to the chandlers and purchase a handheld radio, which I declined to do, much to his frustration. I simply filled up my petrol canisters and left Buckie under power, bound for Gamrie.

The wind had now risen again, but as it was from the South East, I had to continue to use the engine to get home. It had been a long day, so I didn't want any further delay, and sailed straight across Banff bay with my stem pointed straight at Mhor head. It was starting to get a little rough now, although the wind was no stronger than the previous day, the direction meant that I was being splashed with spray from time to time as Lady Too dug in her head to the seas gathering on her starboard bow. I finally entered into Gamrie harbour at 6:00pm, and Andrew was waiting there to help me moor up.

I remember the date well, as it was to be a crucial turning point in my life. It was the 12th September 2008 and when Andrew came down the pier, he remarked to me that a travel company called XL Leisure had gone into administration. My blood ran cold. XL Leisure was the parent company of Travel City Direct, whom we supplied accommodation to in Florida through a USA company called Welcome USA. Welcome USA had become ever slower at paying their bills over the summer, and currently owed us quite a bit of money.

It was late in the season, and I only had one or two sails before taking the boat out for the winter. I had a few sails, mostly with my neighbour Ian alongside, and he gave me some good pointers about sailing. He did have to tow me in one Saturday afternoon when I had problems with the engine. Pearl was none too pleased as we were supposed to be going to Aberdeen that night and as I was late, she had already left and gone without me.

CHAPTER 6

Summer 2009

Summer 2009

After the business took a huge turn for the worse, I had no alternative but to go back offshore to work to make ends meet. I was working adhoc, so had no regular schedule and time at home was taken up looking after a business which was still fairly busy, but firmly in a negative cash flow. The business was to take up a lot of my time and it was really good the few hours I could get to go for a sail and get away from it all into peace and tranquillity.

We were fairly late in putting the boat into the water as Andrew had begun a few jobs, which he never seemed to have time to finish. It was mid-June before we got the boat into the water, and I was away from the 10th July until the end of September with only 2 days at home. The bottom line was that there was very little sailing done in 2009.

I had a few day sails and it was more experimenting with the boat than anything else. The first time I tried to put the cruising chute up, it was a brisk wind and I got a little bit of a scare when the wind took hold of the chute and the boat started to charge away before the wind, even before I managed to secure the sail. In the end, I let the main line go, let the chute fall into the water and I retrieved it by the tacking lines.

On another day, I had a fantastic sail right up to Whitehills, but when I turned to come home, the wind had freshened and I had stiff bounce across Banff bay all the way to Gamrie. On the plus side, I learned that this was a very capable boat, even though she was only 20 feet long.

CHAPTER 7

Summer 2010

Summer 2010

Summer 2010 was the opposite from 2009. I had been fairly busy with work all winter, but at the end of May, the work dried up and I had only five weeks work between the end of May and the following February. This was very stressful, and again it was really good to escape for a few hours from it. Although I had loads of time at home, I was always waiting for a shout for a job, so was not really clear to go away for any length of time.

I did get away one weekend with Johnny, my cousin's husband and good friend, and we had a really good sail up to Lossiemouth on the Friday, with an Easterly wind allowing us to make good progress with the cruising chute getting a great airing.

We left Gamrie in light winds at 7:30am and progress was fairly slow at first. We were even becalmed off Mhor head for a half hour before the wind started to pick up again. The wind was variable and unreliable until mid-day, but in the afternoon, settled into a steady Easterly breeze which saw us berth at Lossiemouth at 4:00pm. The afternoon was particularly enjoyable as we were able to raise the cruising chute, have a fairly fast stable sail in very good sunny conditions.

This was the first time I had stayed overnight on the boat, and although there was not a lot of headroom, it was adequate as long as you were only sleeping in it. The lack of a toilet was a problem, especially if you needed to go during the night, but we could live with it for one night.

In the morning, we were up early, went to the bakers to get some fresh rolls for breakfast before setting sail at 8:00am. The wind had continued from the East, which was not what we really wanted. I had been trying to make up my mind whether we would go to Lossiemouth or Wick the previous day, and as the forecast was for South East winds on the Saturday, I opted for Lossiemouth, as it would be an easier sail home.

Unfortunately, the wind on Saturday was mainly from the East North East, so a sail from Wick would have been much better for us. However, we had chosen Lossiemouth and had no option but to cope with the ENE wind as best as we could. It was a case of tacking all day and by 6:00pm we were only midway between Portsoy and Whitehills. We had both had enough of it, so decided to roll away the sails and complete our journey by engine. It was two very tired sailors who finally sailed into Gamrie at around 9:00pm that night.

That was probably the highlight of 2010 and the remainder of the season were day sails, although I did have plenty of them. I would go out for a few hours, maybe as far as Banff, then back, but I was never settled enough to go any further.

CHAPTER 8

Summer 2011

Summer 2011

By summer 2011, I had the job all sorted out and the business was settling down, even though it was at around 25% of the pre-2008 level of business. I was on a steady 3 weeks on / 3 weeks off rota, and my closest working colleague, Willie Milne, also had a yacht berthed in Whitehills. We had loads of chats over coffee about sailing, and made numerous plans for sailing trips.

We had a number of day sails, separately, and together, but every time we had 3 weeks off, the weather seemed to be majoring from the North, causing an unpleasant swell which curtailed many of our plans.

However, I did start the year with a bang. For my fiftieth birthday, Andrew had given me a week's sailing training, and he would accompany me. Somehow we had just never managed to get this fitted in to our different schedules until late March 2001, when we booked a week with Westbound Adventures, out of Ardrossan, on the Clyde.

We travelled down to Ardrossan on the Sunday night, stayed on the boat, a Sadler 33, overnight, ready to start our training on the Monday morning. I was doing my Coastal Skipper, and Andrew was doing his competent crew member, both RYA approved courses. Monday morning was boat handling in the marina before sailing out into the Clyde in the afternoon.

We sailed out of Ardrossan on Monday afternoon, across to the south end of Bute, where we practiced anchor handling and mooring. There was not a lot of wind and we did some exercises in chart work, manoeuvring and general seamanship, out in the middle of the firth. At night we dropped anchor on the north side of the Small Cumbrae, not having raised the sails at all.

Tuesday morning was not much better, and we motored most of the way up the east side of Bute, through the Kyles of Bute and finished up, late at night carrying out night exercises into Portavadie and West Tarbert, where we moored up at a pontoon for the night. The next morning we all managed to get a shower and a walk up the road before sailing around 11:00am.

We sailed back up through the Kyles of Bute again, and dropped anchor just under the three maids of Bute on the Wednesday night. On Thursday morning, we pulled anchor and started down the North Channel between Bute and Argyll with very light winds. Andrew was getting a turn at the helm when we were hit by a sudden squall, much the same as he and I had experienced in the Beauly firth, and once again, Andrew just about soiled his under garments when the yacht suddenly broached and pulled right round into the wind.

The wind grew from this point, and if they had been too light earlier in the week, they were going to make up for it now. We sailed south and took hold of a buoy in Kilchattan bay, in the south of Bute while we had lunch. Paul, our instructor, now set a choice out before us. We could sail east and moor up in Largs marina for the night, or we could sail south and lay up in Lamlash bay in Arran.

The difficulty with Largs was that the wind was to go into the south east on Friday meaning we may have a struggle returning back to our starting point in Ardrossan, but it would be an easy run there for Thursday afternoon. Lamlash would be an easy run home on Friday morning, but with a force nine currently raging in the Clyde, it would not be an easy run across to Arran from Bute.

We unanimously agreed to head for Lamlash so that we would have an easier run home the next day. Before casting off, Paul instructed us to change the reefing lines, so that he could make use of an extra deep reef he had in his mainsail. With a deep reef in, and a No.2 genoa up, we headed across the open firth and I was surprised how well the boat handled it. It really does go to show that any size of boat can handle rough weather if it is rigged properly.

After completing some man overboard manoeuvres in Lamlash bay, we hooked up to a mooring buoy for the evening and settled down to dinner and a nice final chat before turning in. There were five us including the instructor, one less than a full compliment. While entering into Lamlash bay, we did have one unscheduled event, a grounding, which just goes to show you, broaches and grounding can happen to even the most experienced and qualified of sailors.

While sailing up into Lamlash bay, we were brought up with a sudden jolt. Immediately Paul started the engine and tried to come astern out of the sand, however the boat just would not budge. We tried moving all our weights around and all sorts of things, but to no avail. Paul then asks us to blow up the dinghy, and I thought we would row out and drop and anchor a little further out to pull us out, but Paul said that was not his idea.

I suddenly had a bad feeling that he wanted to lighten the load on the boat, and I knew who was heaviest there. Paul would obviously have to stay on-board to control the boat, and Sue would have been the lightest, being a female. Andrew, I and the other guy (I forget his name), were instructed to board the dinghy to lighten the load on the boat.

We tied the dinghy alongside the boat. I was on one end; Andrew was on the other end with the other guy in the middle. When the yacht suddenly jumped free, my end of the dinghy surged under the water. I was quick to jump up and move to the middle of the dinghy which meant Andrew's end when down, and he found himself soaked up to his waist before he could move. He just wasn't as fast as his old man.

We passed a pretty unpleasant night at the mooring in Lamlash bay in that forward cabin, with the waves continually slapping off the bows, and didn't get much sleep. As expected, we had an easy run across to Ardrossan in the morning, before finishing up at mid-day and heading for home with our certificates. We had a very enjoyable week and learned a lot into the bargain.

In July, I had been home for almost 3 weeks and not been out once. On my last week, I decided I would go and try to have a sail, even though there was quite a bit of motion in the sea. I rose early on the Friday morning and was up in Banff at 6:00am. A quick look out over the North pier confirmed that it was not a very nice day, and that there was a sizeable swell running. However, I decided that I had to get a sail, so made the boat ready and motored out past the pier head.

I rounded the pier head and turned the boat into the swell, trying to assess whether it was a suitable day to continue and which way would be best to go. After trying a few different directions, I decided that there was just too much swell and that it would not be comfortable enough to enjoy a sail, so turned the boat around and headed back into the harbour. That was 3 weeks at home in July and I didn't manage to get out for a sail at all.

On the few occasions when I did manage to get out for a sail, Pearl joined me once, and Jocelyn joined me another afternoon. One hour was about long enough for both of them, and then they wanted back to dry land.

At the very end of August, almost into September, Willie and I had made great plans for a weekend sail, and for once the weather was favourable. We planned to sail up to Lossiemouth on the Friday, back down to Buckie on the Saturday, then home on the Sunday.

I left Banff harbour around 7:00am and Willie was already leaving Whitehills waiting for me. For the first part of the day, we had a fantastic light breeze from the South and we made great progress west to Cullen bay. My little boat was very good on a broad reach and I was racing ahead of Willie's more modern, broad beamed vessel.

As we crossed the bay at Cullen, the wind died away, and despite waiting for it to return, we had, in the end to start up the engine and motor the remainder of the way. We got into Lossiemouth around 5:00pm and tied up at the visitors berth. It is good to have company, and as it was still a decent day, we cracked open a can of beer and kicked back to enjoy the remaining day.

Willie had a small fridge on his boat, so as soon has he had the shore power connected my bottle of baileys was placed to chill in his fridge for later that night. Willie had his bottle of Bacardi at the ready also. We had the obligatory walk up the road to the chippers, and then we returned to the boat to sit in Willie's cockpit at his alfresco table. It was probably one of the best spells of weather we had seen since May, and it was great to sit and watch the world go by while enjoying a few drinks.

In the morning it was a short walk up to the baker's for a fresh bag of rolls for breakfast. There was absolutely no hurry as we were only taking a short sail across the bay to Buckie this day, so we were around 11:00am before we finally cast off and sailed east.

From the point at Lossiemouth to the headland at Portknockie, there is a long curving coastline with one of Scotland's greatest rivers as its centrepiece. The mighty river Spey leaves a huge deposit of silt which ensures good sandy beaches all the way from Portgordon to Lossiemouth, whereas the Eastern side of the Spey is mostly a rocky coastline.

Rather than head straight across the bay, we decided that it would be more interesting to hug the coastline, as far as possible, and see if there were any points of interest we had missed by cutting across this 20 mile bay in the past. I was able to get much closer to the beach than Willie, as he had a single keel, and I had a twin keel boat. The risks involved with running aground in a twin keel boat are minimal, but on a single keel, you don't even want to risk it.

After sailing east from Lossiemouth, we did pass a few dogs and their owners on the beach, but after the first few miles, it was just mile after mile of unspoilt beach stretching up to the treeline and sand dunes. Continuing east, we passed old unused fortifications from WWII days, West of Kingston, designed to hinder any possible invasion by the Nazis.

On to Kingston where two small children played on the beach with their mum and exchanged a cheery wave with me as I sailed past, approaching the mighty Spey entrance. I have seen the Spey further up river and have seen how strong and angry it can be, but at the mouth, certainly on this day, it was a very gentle and mild river.

Once we were east of the Spey, it wasn't long before the coastline changed from Sand to rock, and the first habitation we come to after Spey Bay was Portgordon, a small Banffshire village at one point, but now enrolled into Moray. Portgordon has its own harbour and at one point would have been a very busy fishing port, as were all the small villages along the Moray Firth coastline. Sadly now, these harbours only hold small lobster boats and pleasure craft.

From Portgordon, it is only a short distance to Buckie, the largest harbour between Fraserburgh and Inverness. Buckie was a very important fishing centre with no less than 3 boat building facilities right up into the 1970s. Only one of these remain and then only on a care and maintenance basis. This leaves Buckie the largest harbour in the North of Scotland which has been deserted by the fishing, yet still not really diversified into any other avenue. There are a few cargo ships come in, small oil tankers, a facility for the wind farms at the Beatrice field, but little else.

The only bright spark for Buckie at the moment is the plan to greatly expand the wind farm facility in the outer Moray Firth, and Buckie does seem well placed to benefit from this development. It is rather surprising that they have not converted one of the 4 large basins into a marina, as there is a definite lack of deep water facilities on this coastline. We tied up alongside an old wooden schooner, rather than tying up alongside the unsuitable piers.

We berthed in Buckie at around 3:00pm in the afternoon and were delighted that once again it was a very pleasant day. There was no shore power facility in Buckie, but Willie's fridge had kept its chill well, and my Baileys was deliciously at the right temperature to enjoy. We had another trek up the road to the chip shop before settling down for the night again at Willie's cockpit table.

The wind farm vessel came in and we exchanged a brief wave with David West, the skipper of the vessel, before he headed home for the night. He was out again, early in the morning and was able to give us a weather update before we left port the next morning. Breakfast was extremely cheap. The previous night we had gone into the local Co-operative store and on the bargain shelf, Willie spotted a bag of 4 rolls reduced to 15p as they were out of date the next day. This was the highlight of Willie's weekend, getting these rolls for 3.75p each.

The wind had strengthened a little, so we put a reef in our sails before leaving Buckie in the morning. Once we got outside the harbour, the wind was not as strong as we had thought, so I dropped my reef and hoisted the full sail. The wind was from the South east, so a close reach was the order of the day and Willie's single keel proved its worth against the compromise of a twin keel boat.

We sailed along nicely until we opened up Cullen bay and then the wind strengthened into a moderate breeze, and I would have been happy to have my reef in now. Unfortunately, on my boat, I had roller reefing, and it was more hassle to reef the sail in than it was to live with it, and occasionally have to dump a little mainsail.

All the way east, there are a series of bays from Cullen, Sandend, Portsoy, Boyne then Banff. When I was under the cliffs, it was a pleasant sail, but in the open bay, I had to continually dump sail as the strength of the wind threatened to pull her head upwind. Willie, having a much easier option to reef his mainsail in from the cockpit, raced ahead of me and was into Whitehills and berthed before I passed round Knock head into Banff bay.

All in all, we had a very enjoyable weekend and it just whetted my appetite for more cruising as I began to plan ahead for 2012. I had one more day planned for 2011, mid-September Saturday was regatta day in Banff. I had never entered the boat into any regattas, so thought it would be a good experience. I persuaded Andrew and my nephew Paul to join me for an exciting racing day.

I dropped Andrew and Paul off at Banff to take the boat round to Whitehills, while I went to Whitehills, where the races were starting, to get the race briefing. Andrew and Paul motored round and by the time the briefing was complete, were ready for me to join them. We motored out into the bay and hoisted our sails waiting for the starting signal.

There had been a little wind in the morning, but there really wasn't much now, and as the starting signal was raised we struggled to get across the starting line and get going. Some of the lighter boats raced ahead, but the heavier boats really struggled to get going, many of them abandoning the race, and going back to the next starting line for the next race.

By this point, we were well and truly last in the race, so decided also that we should retire from this race and try the next one. Only problem with that plan was that the engine decided not to co-operate and we could not get it started, despite trying many different things and having 2 trained engineers on board. In the end, we had to get the race marshals to tow us back to Banff, and we had to retire in disgrace from the entire day's proceedings.

I was due offshore again on the Monday, so had no time to do anything with the engine at this point. When I returned home, and tried to start the engine, it started without any problem. I went out for a sail, and when I had to start it to come back in, it performed perfectly. It was an old engine, so I pondered what I would do with it, decided that as I was a sail boat, the engine was only a secondary means of propellant, and I could live with it.

CHAPTER 9

April 2012 Banff to Inverness

April 2012 Banff to Inverness

All through the winter of 2011/2012 I considered the weather we had had for the summer of 2011 and the hankering I had to get more cruising in during 2012. I decided that I would give up my berth in Banff harbour at the end of March 2012 and take the boat through the Caledonian Canal to the West coast. I secured a mooring at Barcaldine Marine in Loch Creran, just north of Oban, and began to make plans for my 2012 cruising season.

The rough plan was to take the boat round to Oban in April, then I would have a 3 weeks at home in May, 3 weeks at the end of June, then another 3 weeks in August, before sailing the boat back home in September. I hoped that I could get 10-14 days cruising in each of those 3 week periods.

I was due off the rig on the 26th of March and had pencilled in to sail on Thursday 29th for the canal, however, as the time approached, I could see that the weather was not going to be very good towards the end of the week, and indeed, if I didn't get away on the Tuesday, it would most likely be another week before I could get away.

I got home to the house around 8:00pm on the Monday evening and immediately started packing everything I needed for my trip. Fortunately, I had already packed many of my things before I went away, so it didn't take me too long. I was up to Macduff for a haircut on Tuesday morning, then a quick run through Tesco for food, and I left Banff harbour around 1:00pm with a plan to keep going all night and get into Inverness before the westerly winds came up.

There wasn't a whole lot of wind that day, so it was going to have to be the outboard engine all the way, and it did seem to be working Ok for now. I left Banff harbour and motored west across Banff bay and round Knock head. My friend, Willie, also had the mind to use the nice day, and had arranged to have his boat lifted in at Whitehills. As he had his boat lifted in, he watched me motor west on my trip.

Whitehills is another of these older fishing ports with only small creel boats left, but in our north east corner, Whitehills have been very proactive in diversifying into the leisure market. They have a great marina, good facilities and a full committee which take an active interest in running the harbour. It is often referred to as being the friendliest marina in the north.

A few miles west of Whitehills, the engine cut out and would not start again. There wasn't a lot of wind, but there was nothing else for it but to put up the sails and try to head west and see how things went. It was very slow going for the next few hours, then the wind did start to pick up in the evening, but it was not a very helpful wind coming from the West.

As you cannot sail directly up into the wind, I had to choose a side to go, and it seemed best to head out into the North-west which slowly took me away from the land all the time. Sailing close to the wind, I was not covering a lot of ground, and I did not want to go too much onto a broad reach. I also wanted to catch a nap, and to do this I had to tie the helm up to keep the boat on its course. It was easier to do this if I held a course as close to the wind as possible.

I lay down in my bunk, fully clothed and set my alarm to go off every 30 minutes, so that I could check around. I needn't have bothered, as every 10-20 minutes, I would feel the boat go away on the wrong course and had to get up and put it back onto the correct course. After around 6 hours of this, I was north of Buckie, but well off the land. My options were to continue on this course and make landfall around the Dornoch firth, then turn and sail south-west along the land to the Beauly firth, or turn now and head south towards Lossiemouth. Inverness or Lossiemouth were the two places I could get a new engine.

I felt that it was not going to be a pleasant trip heading North-west, so opted to turn south and head for Lossiemouth. The weather was not very nice by this time, and I decided it was time to put on my waterproofs. That was when I discovered my waterproofs were still hanging in the garage at home. I had packed in too much of a hurry and forgotten some vital pieces of equipment. I was to get my first soaking of the trip before I managed to get into Lossiemouth at around 11:00am.

I had absolutely no problem in heading into Lossiemouth, as I was now pretty much on a broad reach. My problem now was actually getting into the harbour, as the wind was blowing right out between the two piers, making it impossible for me to sail in there. In the end, I had to seek the help of a local fisherman to tow me in and I was soon tied up again at the visitors berth.

This was my third visit to Lossiemouth, and one of the main reason s Lossiemouth is so popular with visiting yachts is because of the great facilities and deep water access at all tides. Lossiemouth harbour, as we know it today, was originally built in 1837, and then a second basin was added later in the century. The port had always been a very important trading route for the nearby city of Elgin, and was funded by Elgin traders

It was only after the harbour was built, that it attracted a lot of fishermen from other places to resettle there to benefit from the facilities. Like most other fishing ports, Lossie's fishing days are all but over, but the local harbour committee have very successfully diversified into the leisure yachting market and have been the example for all others to follow on the Moray Firth coastline.

A call to James Watt, the local marine engineer, who came originally from our area, secured me a second hand four stroke, 5HP Mariner outboard which had only been run for around 15 hours, and had been retained only as a back-up engine. However, he was away all day, and would not manage to deliver it to me until the following morning.

By this time, I was pretty hungry and was quick to get across the road to the local café and get some hot food in to me. I then went back to the boat and had an afternoon nap. I had been up most of the night, and also I was still in a strange sleeping pattern, having come off night shift only on the Monday morning. I had another feed at the chip shop in the evening before turning in early around 8:00pm.

I was up bright and breezy in the morning as I tend to do when I am just off night shift, and had another trip up to the bakers for my fresh morning rolls and a trip to the local shop for a few more essential items I had discovered I had forgotten. I then had to wait for my engine arriving at 8:30am, before I could head off again. It was not a very nice day, but I was very eager to be off on my way.

James appeared early, around 8:20am and the engine was fitted and I was ready to go before nine. The locals were all telling me it was not a suitable day to go, but I figured it was not going to get any better over the next few days, and I sure didn't want to be holed up here for the next week waiting on weather. The wind was from the West at the moment, but was due to go into the North in the next couple of days, which would mean a build-up of swell, making it even more uncomfortable.

I motored out of Lossiemouth and headed West at half power. It wasn't long before I had my second soaking and was wishing I had acquired some waterproofs in Lossiemouth. I persevered though and inched my way West past Hopeman and Burghead, into that long sweeping Findhorn bay. I headed across the bay, but did keep a little closer to the land than I did in my previous journey here.

Slowly I made progress and was off Findhorn around 1:00pm when the wind freshened to storm force. I was pretty glad I was close to Findhorn so that I was able pop in there and take refuge. I sailed up the river into the wide lagoon. In the hurry, I did not consult my charts and very quickly went aground on the bank in the middle of the estuary. A very helpful guy, I think from the boatyard, came to my rescue in a rib and towed me free. I then moored to a buoy and got out of my thoroughly soaking wet clothes, into a fresh dry change.

Before the development of Lossiemouth as a harbour, Findhorn was the principal port in the Moray Firth and vessels sailed and traded as far away as the Baltic. Unfortunately, Findhorn has a lot of silt and sand which is continually shifting, and as ships started to get bigger, Findhorn was no longer a viable option. Findhorn also played a part in the Jacobite 1745 uprising when the French brigantine Le Bien Trouvé was briefly trapped by two British 'Men O War', too big to enter the bay, awaited for it in the firth. Fortunately, the French ship managed to slip away on a dark night.

A welcome meal was cooked up on my little stove, but it was too rough, even to go ashore in my dinghy. I whiled away the afternoon on the computer, before turning in for another early night around 7:30pm. I was in a sound sleep when Pearl phoned me about 8:30pm, and then just catching again when Willie phoned me around 9:00pm.

As I lay there settling back into my slumbers, I suddenly became wide awake. It wasn't a noise which awakened me, but rather the lack of noise, I became aware that the wind wasn't howling, and that it had become much quieter outside. I rose and popped my head through the hatch and sure enough, the wind had dropped dramatically. I quickly got dressed and had started my engine, dropped my mooring buoy and was motoring out of Findhorn within 5 minutes, heading for Inverness.

The wind was still from the west, there just wasn't as much of it, but it still meant motoring all the way west. The sea was calmer and at least I was staying dry now. I headed west making fairly good progress and consulted my charts to figure out my options. There is a large sandbank at the entrance to the Beauly firth between Fort George and Channonry point. There is a narrow shallow channel to the South which I took on my westward route three and a half years before, and there is a deeper, open channel to the North.

In the dark, I didn't feel confident enough to take the south channel, especially as the weather would have prevented me having my charts in front of me all the time. I headed for the first port hand marker for the North channel, and I could see that red light in the distance. I kept thinking that I was not too far from rounding that marker, but it was well over an hour after first spotting it, that I manage to clear it to port.

By this time, due to the area, the shallow water, the riptides, etc., a very disagreeable short sharp chop had sprung up and was beginning to make the journey a little unpleasant. It seemed to take as long again to work my way through the channel of lights, before I reached the narrow entrance to the firth.

My petrol tank was getting low also, and I certainly didn't want to run out right in the middle of the narrows, so I hove to and topped up my tank from my spare canisters. It was a little more difficult than usual with the boat rolling quite a lot, trying to hold onto my tank on one hand, my torch in the other and not spill too much of the expensive liquid.

I finally got through the narrow channel and came into a calm area where the sea seemed to flatten out. I sensed that something was not quite right, and on consulting my charts, indeed, I had wandered a little from the channel into a small bay at Fortrose. There were quite a lot of lights around, and the very bright lights at Fort George were particularly disturbing, destroying my night vision. I was quite happy to get past them and into the dark again.

The Beauly firth is noted for being a choppy place and it sure didn't disappoint me. Before I made the two hour passage up under the Kessock Bridge, I had earned myself another saturated set of clothes. I was also tired and cold and all in all, it was not the most enjoyable sail I have had, but I got there. At 3:30, I came alongside the entrance to the canal where I would wait for the lock keepers to arrive at 8:00am.

Unfortunately, there was nowhere suitable to tie up at and I had to go back round to the new Inverness marina, where I tied up, got out of my wet clothes and tumbled into my bed, very weary at 4:00am in the morning of Friday 30th of March. Although I had left Banff early, my original plan had been to be waiting for the canal to open on the Friday morning, so I was pretty much back on track.

It had been a rough few days, and my biggest problem was all the wet clothes I had accumulated. The marina had laundry facilities, but I knew of a better laundry in Inverness, one which also served good food. Everyone should have an "Auntie Rosaleen".

I called Rosaleen and Donald when I got up at 8:30am and got all my gear together ready for them coming down for me. I went up to the marina office to register with David Findlay, the marina manager, previously the manager at Whitehills marina, and before that a fisherman working out of Whitehills. The cost was £15 odd for the night, and if I stayed over that night, I would be charged for 2 nights at the full price. I thought that was a bit steep since I only came in at 4:00am, and had he offered a slight discount to £10 for the second night, the marina would have had an extra £10 in its coffers.

In the canal, the minimum licence is for 7 days, so I figured I was better to put the boat in there and use up my 7 days, rather than pay another

£15.00 for a second night in the marina, as I would only be in the canal for three to four days. I planned to go back in the afternoon, enter the canal, take the boat through to Dochgarroch, the last lock before entering Loch Ness, and then go back to Auntie Rosaleen's for a good night's sleep.

CHAPTER 10

Through the Caledonian Canal

Through the Caledonian Canal

After a rest and a good dinner, Rosaleen and Donald took me back down to the boat about 2:00pm and I motored round to the sea lock at Clachnaharry, where there was still quite a bit of jabble around the entrance to the canal. As I entered the sea lock, the lock keeper came down to take my rope, but there was so much jabble, I could not take my attention away from the engine controls to throw up a rope to him. He had to go and shut the outer lock gate first, so that the boat would settle down.

I tied up and went up into the canal office to register and pay for my passage through this magnificent masterpiece of Thomas Telford. For my small 6m boat, the 7 day licence was just over £100, which is a very good rate if you are making full use of the 7 days. If you are only 4 nights, then that works out at a slightly more expensive £25 per night, but still a lot better than sailing through the Pentland Firth and round Cape Wrath.

The business concluded I made my way up the outer canal up into the Muirtown basin. From the Muirtown basin there is a swing bridge and then the "Muirtown Staircase", consisting of 4 locks up to the Caley Marin area. The lock keepers are generally very helpful if you are single handed, especially at this time of year, when they are not too busy.

The swing bridges operate restricted openings at peak rush hour periods, so they advised me that I would not be able to pass through the swing bridge at Tomnahurich until 5:30pm, which was also the stopping time in low season for the canal staff. The bridge operator waited to let me through before knocking off for the night, and I was then able to sail the next few miles up to Dochgarroch and moor up there for the night.

Rosaleen and Donald were a little late coming to pick me up, as some yacht had held them up in long queues at the Tomnahurich swing bridge. I wonder who that would have been. I then got back to Rosaleen's house for another good feed and a relaxing night, before heading down Loch Ness in the morning with freshly laundered clothes.

In the morning, after yet another feed from Rosaleen, we headed down to Tesco's to fill up all my petrol containers, ready to take on the world again. We arrived at Dochgarroch around 10:00am, but I had to wait until a large wood carrying coaster passed through on her way to Corpach. The Kanuta was one of the largest vessels able to transit the canal, and I was later to see her loading her cargo on the Isle of Mull, ready for her trip back up through the canal where she offloaded the wood onto 140 Lorries bound for the pulp mill, just east of Inverness.

I was also tentatively thinking of selling the boat and had a prospective purchaser from Brora coming down to take a look at her. I am not sure what he would have thought, as I had so much stuff in her that the entire forward part of the cabin was unusable and stacked high. At any rate, I never heard from him again, so I guess that tells me what he thought about it.

I finally made it through the lock at Dochgarroch and into Loch Ness. For March, it was a fairly pleasant day, and the only downside was that the winds, although from the right direction, were a little light. I goose winged down Loch Ness on a nice sunny morning, but after 3 hours, I had only made it down to Urquhart castle, and I really wanted to make Fort Augustus and get up through the flight there before night.

Had I not been in such a hurry, Urquhart castle would have made a very interesting stop. This part of the Loch has a very rich history stretching back over 1,500 years. The current castle was destroyed by William of Orange's forces to deny the Jacobites the use of it as a stronghold after their departure. They were very successful in this as the castle has never been rebuilt since.

I started up the engine again and stowed away my sails, making the bottom of the staircase at around 3:30pm, where once again, I held up the traffic at another swing bridge. After I passed through the swing bridge at Fort Augustus, I began my ascent through the 6 locks which are one of the biggest tourist attractions on the canal. Even at this time of year, there were loads of Japanese cameras clicking away as I was moved up the flight where I found the Kanuta waiting on me again.

I moored up at the small pontoon at the top of the flight for the night and went in search of the local watering holes, via the chip shop. The British Legion is very welcoming there and I enjoyed a few drinks with a few of the locals who were very friendly. This was probably the first day of my trip so far which I had been able to remain dry for the entire day.

Although there would always have been some settlement here, Fort Augustus really only came into being when General Wade erected a fort here after the first Jacobite uprising in 1715. It was completed in 1942 and was captured by the Jacobites in 1945, prior to the battle of Culloden, which ended the Jacobite dream.

On Sunday morning, I was up and made myself some porridge and cast off just behind the Kanuta. The last I saw of her for a few hours was as she left the lock at Kytra, and I waited for the next lift to take me ever higher into the canal. The final lift was through the lock at Cullochy which lifted you into Loch Oich, the highest point of the canal passage.

Loch Oich is a small loch with a swing bridge at each end of it. The bridge keepers were fantastic and had the bridge open whenever they saw you coming, allowing you to progress fairly swiftly through the waterways. Loch Oich is a buoyed loch and in a few places there was evidence of boats which had strayed from the channel and come to grief. Loch Oich would not have been deep enough for navigation, but Telford artificially raised the level of the loch when building the canal, to allow it to be used in the system.

At the southern end of Loch Oich is the "Great Glen Waterpark". I had not visited it, and had no time to stop there now, but I am sure it would be a great attraction for the many rental cruisers which ply these waters. From Loch Oich, you pass the swing bridge into the "Laggan Avenue", a beautiful tree lined tranquil two mile stretch through to the first locks which drop you down, at Lagan.

There was a barge at Laggan converted to a restaurant and pub, but it was too early in the year for it to be open. I passed through Laggan locks and tied up to the pontoon while I heated up some soup for lunch, before pressing on down the long Loch Lochy to Gairlochy and the canal down to Corpach.

It was another pleasant sail down Loch Lochy, even though the wind from the south meant I had to use the engine again. The scenery in this part of the route was breath-taking and I thoroughly enjoyed this day's passage on the first day of April. I reached the south end of the loch at 3:00pm and proceeded down the canal to Banavie after passing through the single set of locks at Gairlochy.

When I reached the top of Neptune's staircase at Banavie, the Kanuta was in the bottom lock, stuck there because the swing bridge had broken and would not open. It was too late in the day to descend the staircase, even if I could, so I tied the boat up, plugged in my electrics to charge everything up and headed down to the locally recommended hotel, the "Lochy" for a feed.

Early on the Monday morning, when the canal staff arrived for work, I was advised that the bridge was still not repaired and that it was expected to take a few hours before they would have it operational. I decided to leave my number with them and head into Fort William for a look around.

I walked into Fort William, not quite realising how far it was, but not being in any hurry, I had plenty of time. I walked through the length of the main street and bought myself a pair of waterproof trousers and a hat. I had a bite to eat and a pint before catching the bus back to Banavie. I was just exiting the bus when the canal staff phoned me to let me know that the repair had been completed and that the bridge was now operational again.

I walked up the hill, past Neptune's staircase, a flight of 8 locks and a swing bridge and began to get the boat ready to go to sea. It takes a fair while to descend these locks and I passed the time chatting to two gentlemen from the North-East who were descending the staircase with me. During the descent, a pair of tourists were watching, one of whom I instantly recognized as John McHattie from Macduff, my home town. After we descended, there was a fishing boat waiting patiently at the bottom to go in the opposite direction. It was as well is wasn't high season, or there would have been very long queues after the bridge had been closed for almost 24 hours.

It was a pleasant motor from Banavie down to Corpach, where I took leave of my companions who were staying there for the night, and I exited the sea lock into Loch Linnhe around 4:00pm.

CHAPTER 11

Corpach to Barcaldine, Loch Creran

Corpach to Barcaldine, Loch Creran

Once again winds were light, so I motored down Loch Linnhe to the Corran narrows. This is a narrow restricted stretch of water where the tide runs fast. You cannot pass through here against the tide, in the same way you cannot pass Channonry point except with the tide.

The tide was with me, and I passed through the narrows into lower Loch Linnhe, where the wind strengthened considerably from the South. It wasn't too bad and I could have kept going, but having been able to remain dry for the past 3 days, I really did not fancy getting wet now. I turned the boat to port and edged over towards Kentallen Bay where I intended to drop anchor for the night.

I tried twice to get a hold on the anchor, and in the end I picked up a buoy in the bay. I don't like to pick up a buoy, unless it is marked visitor, as that is someone's property, and maybe they would be annoyed if they looked out of their window and saw you moored to their buoy. Needs must though, and I moored up for the night and settled down for a sleep after a simple meal.

Overnight the wind picked up and turned round to the North. I was not quite so sheltered from this direction, and passed a wild night, where the mooring was never far from my mind. In the morning, the day was none better and it was very clear that I would not be going anywhere that day. It was 9:00am the next morning before I was able to cast off and proceed on my journey.

It was definitely at this point where the decision was made to sell the boat. Being caught in a situation where I was trapped in the boat for 36 hours, there was just not enough room. The biggest problem was the height and not being able to stand up and get dressed, I mostly stayed in my sleeping bag all day and the two nights, only putting on my clothes to go check the ropes.

On the Wednesday morning, it was a much better day, and I cast off at 9:00am and headed down lower Loch Linnhe again. As the wind was still from the North, I was able to hoist my sails and have a leisurely passage down the inside of Shuna Island, past Castle Stalker and into Loch Creran where I was going to keep the boat all summer.

Castle Stalker, mentioned above, is one of the best restored castles in Scotland, due to its unique romantic position on a small island, only accessible at extreme low tide, and with difficulty. The present castle was built by the Stuarts in the 1440s and was renovated between 1965 and 1975. The castle remains in private ownership, but is open to the public.

I moored the boat at 11:30am, but still managed to miss the 1:00pm bus to Fort William, and had to wait a further 4 hours for the next one. The transport to Oban from home was less than satisfactory with a bus to Fort William, another bus to Inverness, a train to Keith before Pearl picked me up for a 30 minutes' drive to Gamrie. This was something I would have to consider. A mooring which had better transport links to the North.

CHAPTER 12

Barcaldine to Loch Liurboist, Isle of Lewis

Barcaldine to Loch Liurbost, Isle of Lewis

Another boat had been in the back of my mind for a while, but truth be told, I was still trying to recover from the financial shock of 2008 and spending money on another boat was not one of Pearl's priorities. Having been trapped in Kentallen Bay for 36 hours in my Vivacity 20 though, was the final straw and whenever I got home, I set about trying to sell the boat and also searching for a new one.

I put the boat up on eBay and set offers quite low, as boats just weren't selling at the moment. There were quite a few folk watching the boat, and one couple from Hopeman, even made the trip down to Oban to take a look at her, while I was offshore. They were fairly excited, but after viewing, came back and said that it was not what they were looking for. Again, they saw it at its worst, packed full of gear.

It did not sell the first time around and I relisted it at the same price. I stipulated in the advert that I wanted to have one last sail during my time off in May, before selling the boat. One young medical student asked if I would incorporate that sail with his need to get the boat home, and also to learn how to sail the boat, and so my final destination for my last sail on Lady Too was destined to be Loch Liurbost in the Isle of Lewis.

To sell the boat so cheap, I had included the old engine, rather than my new one, and I had stripped out all of my extra equipment. When I got home though, James Watt informed me that the old engine was really beyond economic repair. The bearings were rough and these were overheating, causing the engine to shut down after an hour's running, as they expanded. These bearings would need replaced and the cost to do this just was not worth it for an old engine.

I returned to Alastair, the young medical student, who had bought the boat and explained the situation. I gave him 3 options, firstly to pull out of the deal, secondly to pay an extra £400 and get the newer engine, or thirdly to take the boat as it was. He advised me that he would take the boat as it was and that his "Shener" (Granddad in Gaelic) was an engineer and would repair the engine for him.

This did pose another problem in that we would now be sailing to Lewis with an engine which was less than perfect. This was not ideal, but manageable, if I kept the use of the engine for emergencies only, so I decided to go along with it.

I travelled to Oban on the Monday in Andrew's Jeep, so that I would be able to take all my gear home. The trip to Oban included an obligatory visit to Auntie Rosaleen's for lunch in Inverness, of course. I arrived in Oban around 2:30pm and after bringing the boat into the pontoon, from her moorings, I commenced to unload all my gear which was not being sold with the boat into the Jeep.

I had not included the stove in the sale, but as we had to eat on the way there, I left it with the boat, along with a few other essentials, not originally included. I unloaded the new engine and replaced it with the old engine, which was being sold with the boat and then she was finally ready to sail.

Oban, at a population of only just over 8,000, is the largest town between Fort William and the Clyde. Because of its strategically sheltered bay and harbour, it is the starting point for a journey to many of the islands on the west coast of Scotland. In the summertime, the population can swell to over 25,000 as tourists pass through the town. Noticeably, above the town, dominating the skyline is McCaig's Tower, a building which was based on the Roman Colosseum. The elaborate tower was started in 1897, but the owner's death, five years later meant that it was never completed.

Alastair was arriving in Oban around 7:00pm, and we had decided he would leave his car there, so that there was transport ready when we came back off the return ferry, and I would leave the Jeep out at Barcaldine Marine, our mooring place, which was about 12 miles north of Oban. I travelled into Oban a little early and had my usual chip supper while I waited for Alastair to arrive, then it was back to Barcaldine Marine to let Alastair view his vessel.

Alastair was happy enough with it, and so we were clear to set sail for Lewis the following morning. We bedded down for the night and were up fairly early in the morning, casting off from the pontoon around 6:00am. There was a Westerly wind and we were able to sail on a close reach across Loch Crerran and out into Loch Linnhe at a reasonable pace. After exiting Loch Crerran, we sailed down the east side of Lismor to the foot of the Sound of Mull.

When we reached the foot of the Sound of Mull, there was a storm raging down through the sound, making it impossible to sail up there. We turned and ran back up the East side of Lismor to a collection of small Islets where we could drop anchor and wait a little. There was an anchoring place marked on the chart, just to the North of the island closest to Lismor, and so I decided to drop anchor there and we would heat up some soup for lunch while we decided what we would do next.

We dropped the anchor, but not having an engine available to bed it in was not very handy. It did seem to be holding though and we weren't moving, so went below to heat up some Heinz tomato soup. An hour later, as we were eating our soup, I voiced some concern to Alastair that we were not holding our position, and agreed that we would pull the anchor as soon as we were tidied up after lunch.

We barely got tidied up before it became evident that the anchor was no longer holding and that we were now drifting fairly fast. We got the forward genoa out and turned the boat round in an attempt to pull the anchor, but we were now becoming dangerously close to the next island and its rocky westerly face. This was definitely one of those times of emergencies when we needed to start the engine, and to my relief, it started almost first kick.

We were so close that I had to fend the boat off the rocks with my pole, while I ran the engine full astern and pulled us away from the island. It was a very close thing, and certainly taught me a lesson about choosing an anchoring position in the future. I had thought that we would be OK as we were only anchoring there for a short time and would not be going to bed, but I think the clear lesson is, never anchor where the wind can blow you down onto a dangerous shore.

When we finally got the anchor up, it was a real mess of weed, and it took Alastair a little while to get it all cleared while I got the boat to safety. Once clear of the island, I stopped the engine and reverted to wind, which, unfortunately today, there was plenty of. We headed south again, testing the Sound of Mull, kept going across it, and then tried to get up into Loch Speive on the Island of Mull.

We tried to tack up into Loch Speive, but after a few hours, it was obvious we were making little progress. We decided to take a chance on running the engine for a while to help us get up past the narrow part of the loch, where we would then have a better opportunity of manoeuvring under sail. Again the engine started no problem, but this was to be the last time we were to have the engine available to us, and we would have done better to preserve it for an emergency.

In the end, we were unable to get up into Loch Speive and we turned and came down the loch much faster than we had gone up it. We headed north towards the Sound of Mull again where the wind had eased down a little. At around 10:00pm, at the entrance to the Sound, I sent Alastair off to bed and told him I would call him around 2:00am to take over and let me get a rest.

I tacked up the sound and was able to make some progress while the tide was in my favour, however I was fully aware that the tide would be turning around 4:00am and we would then struggle to get anywhere at all. As I had been able to make some progress, I decided that I would head over in the direction of Craignure, where would try to get alongside the pier and tie up for the 6 hours ebb tide.

As I got closer to Craignure, I would lose the wind, making it very difficult to get alongside the pier. At one point, in the dark, I came too close to an out crop of land and went aground on the sandy bottom. This was around 2:00am and I got Alastair up to help me get her off the bottom and back out from the land a little. It would have been no problem at all with an engine, but we could not get it to start, so only had the sails available, and a set of oars.

The oars were handy for reaching down and propelling ourselves like a gondola, while we were in the really shallow water, but once out into the deeper water, we struggled to row against the tide with the weight of the boat. We managed to get the boat back out a little, where we picked up a little more wind, getting further West in the sound, before making another attempt to get into Craignure.

At times we were so tantalizingly close to the pier, it was tempting to jump in and swim ashore with a rope, but we drifted past yet again. I think it was our fourth attempt, and around 4:00am, when we finally managed to catch the ladder at the North end of the pier and get a rope ashore. We pulled the boat around and moored up for the night and went below for a sleep.

I never sleep very well, when there are things on my mind, and so I was up at 8:00am again and up to the local shop for some fresh supplies. After a quick breakfast and a coffee, we were ready again to head out into the sound to catch the flood tide which would help carry us west. The wind, although not so strong, was still coming down the sound from the west, so it was not going to be an easy day up to our target of Tobermory.

All day we tacked back and forth while all sorts of vessels motored up past us. The big Cal Mac ferry headed for Loch Boisdale in Uist, large ore carriers from the quarry at Glensanda, specialized fish farm boats heavily laden heading east to Oban, then conspicuously empty heading west a few hours later, small fishing boats and even many other yachts who had decided to motor rather than try to fight the wind. Further up, we also spied the Kanuta loading wood at a terminal on the North side of Mull.

It was a pleasant enough sail though and we finally entered into Tobermory bay around 6:00pm that evening. The visitors buoys were well inside the bay, but having no engine, we opted to moor well out, where it was easier to get to, and more importantly, easier to get away from in the morning. It did mean a longer row in our little dinghy, but that was unavoidable.

Rowing in the dinghy had also become a little harder, as we had discovered after our little anchoring mishap that we had lost one of our oars. We had searched a little for it, but had been unable to find such a small object in the vast sea. We were down to one paddle, but still managed to row ashore and take advantage of the facilities available in Tobermory.

Thinking about all the ports I had been into, and indeed, even since then, Tobermory has the best facilities for yachts I have seen. The toilets and showers were excellent and we enjoyed a nice hot shower and a change of clothes before checking out the local restaurants for my first decent meal since Auntie Rosaleen's. After a meal and a couple of drinks, we headed back to the boat where we bedded down for the night.

I woke around 5:30am and stuck my head out of the hatch to see what the weather looked like. It was a "mochy" day, as we would say in the North-east, which means it was a damp drizzly wet day. However, the wind had turned round into the South-east, so I wasn't going to waste that and very quickly pulled on my clothes and was up on deck and underway before 6:00am. I told Alastair to go back to sleep and get up when he was fully rested. I was rounding Ardnamurchan point; two and a half hours later, when the hatch finally slid back and he looked out into a miserably wet day.

We had made really good progress out to Ardnamurchan point, the most westerly point on the British mainland, but once we rounded the point, the wind was on our stern and these Bermudan rig sail boats don't perform so well before the wind. At this point, I wished I had brought my cruising chute, but I had quite enough to carry back on the ferry with me, especially the big bulky dinghy, which we just couldn't have managed without.

A couple of hours later, as we headed north-east towards the Sound of Sleat, two undesired events began to unfold. The wind started to drop and the rain began to get heavier. Our plan was to head through the Sound of Sleat to somewhere in the region of Kyle of Lochalsh, or alternatively, if not progressing so well, to head into Mallaig. As the wind had dropped, we were making very slow progress towards Mallaig, and being soaking wet through and through, just wanted to get out of this weather as fast as possible.

We decided to turn and run into Eigg, one of the "Small Islands", and tie up there for the night. We weren't sure what facilities there were there, but just hoped that there would be laundry facilities to dry our clothes. Again as we neared Eigg, the shelter from the land stole all the wind from our sails and we struggled to get alongside. It was very slow, but we did manage at the first attempt, and tied up alongside the pier around 3:00pm.

We were glad to find purpose built visitors facilities at the head of the pier and enjoyed a lovely hot shower and a change of clothes, perhaps not fresh, but at least dry. Unfortunately, there was no laundry facilities and we ended up hanging up our wet clothes in the small shelter at the end of the pier for waiting ferry passengers. With only eighty residents on the island, I don't think it was used very much.

We made our way back up to the visitor's centre where there was a shop and a café, neither of which was currently open. A few of the locals appeared, and being a small place, they had keys to the café, and were able to secure us a few cans of beer. They were very friendly and one resident even insisted in buying us our first drink. Another local, Donna (http://www.donnathepiper.co.uk), appeared with her bagpipes and when another 4 sailors appeared off a fast rib, a party was underway.

I got chatting to the other sailors and discovered I had worked with one of them, Bob Galbriath, 16 years previously, on board the Maersk Vinlander. A bunch of Kayakers wandered in and the party was going well in Eigg. This was most definitely the most hospitable spot I had visited and will certainly be back here again.

The locals eventually disappeared, the four guys from the fast rib, took off for Knoidart where they had booked a table at the "Old Smithy", famous for being the most remote pub on the British Isles. The Kayakers retired to their tents for the night, leaving Alastair and I the only ones who remained, both taking advantage of the decent Wi-Fi connection available here.

There was a huge tidal drop here and when we returned to the boat, it was high and dry in the harbour which was completely dried out. We bedded down for the night and rose around 8:00am in the morning to find out that the rain at least, had stopped, and the wind had freshened up a little from the North. We would have been able to leave at this point, but decided we would wait until the café opened at 10:00am for breakfast, and then catch the next tide at around 3:00pm.

Had we known the menu and quality, we would most likely have gone earlier. We both felt that the choice and quality of the food was disappointing, especially as we were really looking forward to a good feed before we headed off again, not knowing when we would next have a square meal.

The one thing in the favour of this island was the friendliness and helpfulness of the locals, and figuring out that it would be difficult for us to get out of the harbour, due to the northerly winds, one of the locals offered to tow us out into the bay. This was a great help to us and around 3:00pm, we cast off his rope in the bay, and headed through the South entrance to the island's anchorage point, and along the south coast of Eigg.

We crossed over and sailed along the South-coast of Rhum, and as the day was wearing late, decided to turn north into Canna for the night. There was still a fresh breeze blowing from the North and we had to tack a few times to get through the sound between Rhum and Canna. We eventually picked up a buoy, at the second attempt, around 8:30pm and rowed ashore to find out what Canna had to offer.

In short, not a lot. There was only a population of twelve on the island, there was no mobile phone signal, and the only public telephone was currently out of order. We met a fellow sailor at the pier as we pulled our dinghy up, and he pointed out a restaurant to us, about ½ mile away. He did advise us to be quick though, as it closed about 9:00pm

A Dutchman was the proprietor here, and he quickly advised us that we were too late for a meal, but that he would be able gives us soup, sandwiches and a sweet, if we wanted. The quality of the food here was definitely much better than Eigg, but unfortunately for me, it was very upmarket and fancy, which I just don't do, as anyone who knows me will be aware of. I ordered the soup, but couldn't eat it, so settled on the ham sandwiches and an absolutely delicious toffee sweet. Again those who know me will be aware that I rarely turn down a sweet.

It was now Friday night, and we headed back to the boat and turned in for the evening. The morning brought us a decent enough day with the wind still coming from the North, but suitable enough for us heading North-west to round Skye. We dropped the mooring buoy and sailed out of Canna, not a place I would hurry back to, unless I was specifically looking for a sheltered, secure mooring place to ride out a storm, and set a course for the Westerly tip of Skye.

The wind was very favourable and we made very good progress towards Skye and rounded the South-west point around mid-day. As often happens, coming close to the land, changes the wind you get in your sails, and on this occasion, we began to lose the wind and progress was slowed dramatically. We made very slow progress up the West coast of Skye, but it was an absolute cracker of a day and we kicked back and enjoyed the glorious sunshine.

In the early evening, everything just seemed to come together to make it a perfect day. The sea was flat calm and there was no wind, so we weren't moving much, but there was wall to wall sunshine, it was warm and the Dolphins had come out to play. There were a shoal of, must have been around two hundred, dolphins playing with us, and had they been much closer, they would have been inside the boat. Alastair captured the scene in a small movie clip on his iPad.

We decided that whatever way the winds and seas played out, we would keep going all night, while it was decent weather to cross the Minch. The Minches can be very dangerous and when you get a decent chance to cross them, in such a small boat, you take it.

I went below to conjure up some food and we had a most enjoyable meal consisting of tinned Chunky Chicken, marrowfat peas and Smash. It tasted all the better eating alfresco out in the cockpit. A nice Baileys rounded off the meal just perfect.

Alastair had been around boats all his life, but had never sailed before, but by this point in the journey, he had picked up all the important aspects of sailing and was fairly competent to become the owner of this wee boat, which we would be delivering to his home port in less than 24 hours. It was time for me to start handing over the control to him and leave him to make the decisions.

Jointly we decided to set 3 hour watches and keep sailing as best as we could through the night. I would take the first watch, from 9:00pm until midnight, and then Alastair would take over until 3:00am. Progress on my watch was fairly slow, but when I got back up at 3:00am, Alastair had her running nicely on a broad reach, and we were well out across the Little Minch. By the time Alastair came back up at 6:00, we were closing on the Chiants and I handed control over to him for the final time.

His local knowledge guided us safely into Loch Liurbost to the slipway just below the Church of Scotland around 9:30am on the Sunday morning. Those of you from the Western Isles will know that a Sunday is not the day to be doing this type of thing, and so there was a rush to get the boat moored up and away before the kirk folk started to appear. I quickly unloaded all my belongings and left the boat to Alastair and his father who moored it to a buoy out on the bay.

After 5 days at sea, I was looking forward to the famous island hospitality, and could almost taste that big feed that Alastair's family would have waiting for us. That is the way it would have happened with us at home, and I figured that the islanders would still pretty much live that way, so I was more than a little disappointed when I was offered a sandwich and a cup of coffee.

Alastair's dad gave me a lift down to Leverburgh where I could catch the ferry across to Uist. They advised me that as I left the ferry at the other side, a bus would be waiting which would take me all the way down to Loch Boisdale where I could catch the CalMac ferry back to Oban in the morning. When I reached the other side, I was to discover that no bus ran on a Sunday, so there was no way for me to get down to Loch Boisdale unless I could find a taxi.

Fortunately, I was overheard talking to the attendant on the ferry, and a very helpful fish merchant offered to take me down to Loch Boisdale if I didn't mind the smell in his fish van. I hadn't had a shower since leaving Eigg, so I reckoned the fish van couldn't smell any worse than me, and accepted his kind offer.

I arrived in Loch Boisdale and managed to secure the last room at the Loch Boisdale hotel which is right next to the ferry terminal. I ordered some food at the bar, and headed upstairs for a shower and shave while it was being prepared. After a hearty meal and a couple of pints, I retired for the evening before catching the ferry early in the morning, long before the hotel started serving breakfasts.

A very helpful steward watched me approach the gangplank of the ferry on the Monday morning and rushed to help me climb the 20-30 feet up to the entrance to the vessel with my huge load. I had my back pack with all my clothes and my laptop, another waterproof bag with more clothes and of course, my dinghy, which felt like it weighed a ton.

I settled into the boat to enjoy a trip to Oban via Castlebay on the islands of Barra, the southernmost group of islands in the Western Isles. I do love to see new places, and it was good to go via Castlebay, and I have added it to my list of places to visit at some point in my next boat.

After an uneventful trip back to Oban, I again struggled along the pier with my bags, stopping often to rest along the four hundred metre route to the bus stop. It is fortunate that I did not stop for longer periods, as I had no sooner arrived there than the hourly bus came along and I was quick to board and head out to Barcaldine Marine where the bus service terminated.

I unloaded all my bags at the roadside and figured it would be easier to bring the jeep to them rather than lug all my heavy load to the Jeep. I got on my way, headed home to Gamrie, of course, via Auntie Rosaleen's to see how the old folks were doing.

That was the end of "Lady Too" and now the search for a new boat was on. I was in no particular hurry as the following trip at home; we had booked a holiday in another set of islands, but in much warmer climes. Next trip at home, we were off to the Greek islands. Who knows, maybe a boat out there would be a better idea. Pearl doesn't think so!!

PART 3

Punto di Svolta

Part Three – Punto di Svolta

CHAPTER 13

The educated search

The Educated Search

I had almost 4 years under my belt now as a yacht owner, if the "Lady Too" was grand enough to be called a yacht, and I had pretty much figured out in my mind what I wanted in my next boat. I had had enough of outboard engines and I also really did not like the noise they made, so an inboard diesel engine was a priority.

The new boat had to have decent headroom so that I could at least stand up if I was staying on the boat for a prolonged period, have a proper table to sit down at with my laptop and keep in touch with the world. I also wanted a proper toilet compartment, although I would settle for a chemical toilet. Beyond that, I was fairly open to the boat I would buy, but price did restrict me a little, as I was still not exactly flush with cash.

I had been looking around for a few months, and had pretty much fixed on the Pegasus 800 as a type of boat which answered all my requirements, but was still available at a very reasonable price. The Pegasus 800 and Pegasus 700 had been built by Ridgeway Marine in Lowestoft from 1977 until the 1990s, so would still be around a thirty years old boat. In all reviews the boat was also commented as being spacious and moderately fast, which sounded good to me.

My own boat had gone cheaply, around half of what I had paid for it, but I knew that whatever boat I bought, in the current market, would also be cheap. Boats were a luxury and in the present economic climate, not many people were thinking along those lines. Boats were difficult to sell, and I could take my pick.

I had watched a nice clean example of a Pegasus 800 down in Wales being offered on eBay over the course of a few months with the offer price being reduced from £7,900 down to £6,900. It was a really nice boat, well looked after, and I very nearly went for it. The only thing that put me of was that it had a hank on fore sail instead of roller reefing. To fit roller reefing would cost at least £500.

There was another Pegasus 800 down in Felixstowe which looked like it had been neglected a bit, but was considerably cheaper at £5,750. Well-kept Pegasus 800s had been selling up to £12k prior to the recession and at some point; I guess they would go back to that price. Early on, when I wasn't really ready to buy, before I had delivered the "Lady Too", I had submitted a cheeky offer for this boat of £3,500. It was no surprise when it was turned down, but now that I was ready to buy, I revised that offer up to £4,500 which the owner countered with a price of £5,250 which I agreed to, on the basis I would pick it up on the 1st August.

In the photographs on the broker's website, it was very clear that I would have a lot of work to do on this boat, but given that I wanted to change quite a few things on even the better kept boat, it did make more sense to go for the cheaper boat and then get it up to my requirements with the cash I had saved. The difference between the prices of the two of them was £1,650, which was a fair bit of cash.

I was a little disappointed to see the nice one in Wales being further reduced to £6,200 a few weeks later and thought that perhaps I had just been a little too hasty in tying up this deal. Of course, you may remember away back at the beginning of the book, in my background, I did warn you that I was a little impatient and impetuous.

I had my boat, and the only difference between the two were a good clean, recover the seating and overhaul the engine, so I guess that would pretty much cover the price difference. The one in Felixstowe had a proper toilet, where the one in Wales only had a chemical toilet, so that was a plus.

CHAPTER 14

The purchase and planning

The Purchase and Planning

I had tied up the deal well in advance and was required to place a deposit, part of which would be non-refundable due to the longer time frame in the deal being completed. As I was buying through a broker, it was fairly safe and the broker held the funds until I picked up the boat and was happy with it. There was a bit of paperwork to complete, but all in all it was fairly smooth and working through a broker helped tremendously.

The deal all tied up, the paperwork done; the focus was now on getting the funds in place and planning the pick-up and delivery of the boat home to the North-east of Scotland. Felixstowe was around 440 miles from Gardenstown, so it would be the longest journey I had undertaken to date.

I had a number of things to think about. Firstly, who would come with me, or would I have to sail it home alone. I would have no problem sailing it home alone, but it may just take a little longer, but having three weeks off, that was not a huge problem. Johnny, my cousin Mary-Ann's husband offered to go with me, so that was at least company. Johnny has some health and mobility issues since he had a stroke a few years back, but he never let that stop him trying, and lived life to the full, but due to his restricted mobility, would be limited in his usefulness.

Nearer the time I managed to persuade Douglas Murray, our local retired baker and a good friend to come along. Neither of these two had a lot of experience in sailing, or indeed boats of any type, so the full responsibility would still lie on me with only minimal back up. I also posted a bulletin on the rig and one guy, Scouse Dave agreed to come, however, on the day he was a no show and it was just down to the three of us. That was the crew in place, so now to draw up a plan for the trip.

I booked my train ticket to Felixstowe well in advance and was able to get a ticket for only £45. At this point I still did not know who was coming with me, so was only able to book the one ticket. Later when Douglas agreed to accompany me, he had to pay £70 for the exact same ticket. Johnny also booked a ticket to join the train at Edinburgh, and so our passage to Felixstowe was all organized.

The grand plan was to travel to Felixstowe on Wednesday the 1st August, two days after I got home from the rig. We would arrive there around 6:30pm and the broker would take us to inspect the boat and conclude the final paperwork, if I accepted the boat. It would have to be pretty bad before I did not agree to proceed, given we had all travelled over 400 miles to sail it home.

Other than inspect the boat, we would not do much that night, other than make the boat suitable for bedding down for the night. In the morning, we would clean up and do any work required on the hull, including renaming the boat, before having it launched. I had ordered a new name for the boat online, as I did not fancy keeping the current name of "Passing Wind". Incidentally, the yard people told me his small tender was called "Little Fart".

We had agreed that the yard people would anti-foul the boat before we arrived and after inspection they would launch the boat for us, all within the price paid for the boat. Hopefully we could get the boat launched around midday, but we had plenty of work mapped out for ourselves in getting the boat ready and cleaned up anyway, that the exact timing wasn't important.

We would allow ourselves the entire day on Thursday to get the boat ready and then hopefully sail on the Friday morning tide around 9:00am. The exact stops on our journey would be determined by our progress and the weather, but it was hoped that we could make Hartlepool on the Sunday and stop there overnight. There were pretty good marina facilities there where we could get a wash and even launder our clothes.

From Hartlepool we would take a further two days up to Eyemouth or Dunbar, where Johnny would leave us, as he had a pre-arranged appointment he had to attend. Douglas and I would continue homeward, arriving on Friday the 10th, with possible stops at Arbroath and Peterhead. That was the rough plan, but as you have read over previous chapters, planning is OK, but reality is seldom as straight forward.

In between the planning and the execution, Pearl and I had a holiday booked to Athens, then to Naxos Island. I also had a course to complete for my work. All this time, I am just thinking, I want to get away and pick up my boat. The waiting and expectation was with me at all times, and I would sit and just look at the pictures of the boat on my computer screen saver many times in the day. However, the allotted time did arrive and I finally got off the rig and home late at night on the 29th August.

The next day was a blur, pulling all my bits and pieces together while also trying to sort through and answer 3 weeks of mail. I needed quite a lot of gear with me, quite apart from my normal clothes and sleeping bag. As the winds were mainly going to be from the South, I would need my cruising chute, which I had not sold with the last boat. As far as I knew, this boat only had a forward sail and a mainsail. I would also need my toolkit with me, as I may have some repairs to make enroute. A couple of empty diesel cans would be essential, as would my waterproofs and my two lifejackets. If there were no more lifejackets on the boat, then I would have to buy a third one.

As we were travelling fairly early in the morning of the first, we agreed to go through to Aberdeen and stay the night with Andrew and Natalie and Andrew would take us to the station first thing in the morning. All this went according to plan and we were finally on our way to Felixstowe. Talking to Johnny, it transpired he had booked the wrong train, and the train he had booked from Edinburgh was an hour later than when our one passed through. No big problem though, as we had an hour to wait in York, so we would meet up then and be on the same connection.

Douglas and I managed to grab some dinner at York while we waited, and we met up with Johnny and all got onto the same train heading south again. We had two more scheduled changes, one at Peterborough and another, with a half hour wait at Ipswich. Since the broker stayed in Ipswich, he agreed to pick us up there, saving us the final leg of our train journey. There was a small delay on the train from Peterborough, but nothing major, and we duly arrived and met the broker at Ipswich only a little late. We filled up his people carrier to the brim with our entire luggage and headed for Felixstowe to view the boat.

The boat was in a yard in an area which was actually called "Felixstowe Ferry", or by some, "Old Felixstowe", which was situated two miles to the north of the main town, close to the mouth of the river Deben. There were a lot of boats here and a number of small sheds sold their produce to tourists and locals who seemed to be plentiful. There were also a number of small eating places around, and that would be very helpful for us.

When we arrived, the yard was closed and the gate was barred to motor traffic. We left the car at the gate and went to inspect the boat. Externally it was pretty much as I expected, needing a lot of work, but nothing I couldn't handle, or pay someone to handle. Inside was a little different, and although I did not expect five star luxuries, I was rather appalled at the filthy mess the boat had been allowed to get into. There was no way we would manage to stay there that night, and indeed, everything in the boat would have to be thrown out, as it was just filthy.

I accepted the boat and got the final paperwork sorted out. It appeared that it was the yard that owned the boat, and I can only assume that they fell heir to it due to the current economic downturn and just wanted to get rid of it. They certainly were making no effort to present the boat in a good way, it was just lying there deteriorating and being neglected.

Now we had to get somewhere to stay the night, and the broker dropped us off back in the centre of the town before we parted company. We tried a number of hotels and guest houses before we were able to secure rooms for the night. Some had one room available, but as there were three of us, which was no good to us. Finally we found one along the front with one single and one twin, and we settled for that, Douglas taking the single and Johnny and I sharing the twin room.

After settling in and freshening up, we headed out for a meal. We found a local sit down chip shop and had a passable meal, although nothing special. We returned to our hotel, had a quick drink, and then off to bed, agreeing to meet for breakfast around 7:30, before going to Morrison's superstore to buy everything we needed for the boat. We had left everything except our clothes on the boat, so did not have so much luggage now.

As it transpired we were up at Morrison's around 8:30am, only to find that it did not open until 9:00am, which we though very strange for a major supermarket. The taxi had dropped us off and we had no option but to wait until the store opened. In addition to food supplies, we bought plates, cups, cutlery, pots and pans, cleaning products, plenty of them, dish towels wash cloths, tin openers, ladles, glasses and loads of other things. We bought everything we would need on the boat, as we intended to throw out everything already in the boat at the moment.

It was well after 10:00am when the taxi finally dropped us back at Felixstowe Ferry and we lugged all our purchases up to the boat. The priority was now to get the hull work done so that we could launch the boat. We could start the interior clean up once we were in the water tied up alongside. I removed the old name from the boat and cleaned up the area of the hull where the new name would be going. It was a big area, as I had chosen a longish sort of name, "Punto di Svolta".

The name is Italian and means turning point. After the events of the previous four years, I was looking, and indeed, believed I was at a turning point in my life, hence the name. The past four years had given me a different outlook in life and had forced me to examine the important things in life. I had been so busy over the previous thirty years; I had never followed my dream of owning a yacht. That was now changing, and I was coming to realise, more and more, it was now or never, and in another twenty years' time, the opportunity would have passed.

We got the hull all cleaned up, the name added and in general, from the outside she was looking pretty good. We still hadn't done anything inside, but decided that some lunch was in order first. We had discovered that once launched, we would have to go onto a buoy as there was no place to come alongside safely in this very fast flowing river. In light of this, it seemed best to have some lunch before we launched the boat and had a more difficult route to the hotel.

We had a nice lunch at the Ferry Inn which had a history as a hostelry going back around 400 years. We the proceeded to launch the boat and get it onto a mooring buoy. Once launched and secured to a buoy, I began an initial check of the boat. On opening the engine compartment, I discovered water flooding in through the sea cock from which a hose had obviously been removed and not replaced. Luckily, the sea cock was in good condition and easily shut off until we were able to get a replacement hose.

Once we replaced the hose, we tried to start the engine, but it just would not start. The guy from the yard tried too, but he also could not get it to start. Unfortunately, their engineer was on holiday that week and was not available; however after contacting him, following his advice, and the engine still not starting, he agreed to come out first thing in the morning to get us up and running.

That was a little disappointing, as we had been planning to just get going that evening around 7:00pm and catch the north flood tide, and get half a day ahead of our schedule. Couldn't be helped though, and we settle ourselves to stay the night. We got the boat all cleaned up and made it habitable, and although the yard had given us a tender to get ashore, Johnny and Douglas did not want the hassle of using a tender in this fast flowing river, and we decided just to heat up some soup for our dinner that evening.

CHAPTER 15

Felixstowe to Scarborough

Felixstowe to Scarborough

We were up and made breakfast long before the engineer appeared at 9:00am, and everything on the boat was ready to go as soon as the engine was fixed. We had topped up the diesel tank and our two spare canisters which would allow us up to 96 hours motoring at cruising speed. As is usually the case, when the engineer appeared, he had the engine running in only 5 minutes, and we wasted no time in saying our goodbyes and motoring down the river Deben.

We had to sail a fair bit extra south just to clear the sand banks at the entrance to the estuary but we were finally out into the open sea and on our way home. On an inspection the previous day, I had actually discovered 5 sails on the boat, not the two I was expecting. The boat had a No.1 Genoa, a No. 2 Genoa, a storm jib, a main sail and another which I have not yet discovered what it is.

I got out the mainsail and rigged it up on the boom, ready to hoist. I also dug out the No.2 genoa, simply because it looked in the best condition, and hanked it on forward. I did not hoist it, as the wind being on our stern, I decide we would make much better progress with the cruising chute. I got out my own cruising chute, hoisted it and then the mainsail, and we began to fly along to the north.

We made fantastic progress that day, and I was really pleased as we sailed up past Lowestoft, where this boat had originally been built, around 5:00pm, a distance of about 35 miles in 7 hours. Along this coast, there weren't many places you could berth and so it was decided that we would keep going all night, heading north, while the going was good. Towards the evening, the wind dropped and shifted round, and so I took down the cruising chute and put up the Genoa. Johnny and Douglas did not have the experience for a night watch, so the night shift was down to me and I would get a rest in the morning, hopefully.

We progressed pretty well and cleared the Norfolk coast around 8:00pm. We were now into the Wash, and it was a bit of open sea across to the Humber area. I sent the guys down below and settled myself into a night watch, wrapped up against the chill of the night. I peered at the compass which was in a terrible filthy mess, and remembered the new compass I had down below and made a mental note to install the new one the next day.

One of the jobs I need to do was to add an inverter to the boat to allow me to charge up my battery based electronics. At this point, I had always used my mobile phone for my charts and GPS, and it worked well enough, but my battery had gone flat on me, and when I went to put in the spare battery, I discovered it was flat too. I was sure I had charged them all up before leaving home, but that was no good now.

The compass was reading 310 degrees and I could see quite a lot of lights away in the distance, so although I could not tell my exact location, I had a fair idea that this was the direction I wanted to head in. I did have the laptop down below which I could use for a backup, but didn't want to disturb the guys sleeping, so kept going towards the lights.

As I neared these lights, they turned out to be a wind farm, and there weren't a whole lot of lights behind them as I would have expected in the

Humber estuary. I had never been in this area before, so was not too sure of the layout. There was a headland with the wind farm just off this, so I turned to starboard, along the coastline there, assuming that the open area to the south was the entrance to the Humber.

It was now daylight and Johnny and Douglas appeared on deck. I was getting pretty tired and I left them to generally follow along the coast line, and I would go below for a sleep. I went below around 8:00am and was back up on deck around 10:00am to observe us still sailing along the coastline and in the distance I could see a large headland. This must be Flamborough head, so I was very pleased with the progress we had made.

We came up alongside Flamborough head around lunch time and this is the first time when I began to get the feeling that something wasn't quite right. As we rounded Flamborough head, we ran into some sand banks, and had to make a huge detour out to sea to get clear of them. Of course, I didn't have my electronic charts and GPS, but on the paper chart, although it was in quite a large scale, I just could not reconcile this with what we were seeing.

We kept going and were rounding this headland, although well out to sea. Johnny was at the tiller and I asked him which direction he was going. Of course, the compass was not much use and he estimated we were heading north. A glance at the sun, which was now beginning to come out, confirmed my suspicions that something was not right. It was now 2:30pm and the sun was slightly on our starboard side. Any seaman will pretty quickly figure out that this means we were heading south.

I told Johnny to turn the boat around and head into the North-west until I could figure out what was going on. There appeared to be a large sweeping bay, and away to the North West, more lights appeared as we sailed in that direction at nightfall. Consulting the chart, I figured that these would be some of the towns to the north of Flamborough head and if I get going in that general direction, I would eventually come to Scarborough or Whitby, where we could berth up for the day.

We continued in this general direction, still being plagued with sand banks, so having to keep well out from the land. During this time of sand banks, we must have sucked some sand up into our intakes and the engine overheated and we got an alarm. I shut the engine off as a precaution, and started it up again after a half hour break. This happened a few times, and then at one point, the engine simply refused to start again.

Being so far out from the land, it was difficult to determine what the lights were as it started to come down dark, but I did seem to be near a pretty big place, and coming in fairly close, it did not look like a place I could enter, so I kept going towards more lights I could see in the distance. As I passed this first place, I was treated to a display of fireworks similar to what I had seen at Disneyworld, Florida, so I figured that this was a holiday resort, but still wasn't too sure which one.

All up and down the east coast of England there were holiday resorts and my thinking was that this was Filey and that he lights I could see in the distance would be Scarborough. I sent the guys off to bed again and I kept watch through the night heading towards Scarborough. I passed the next set of lights which weren't much, and kept going trying to figure out in my head what was going on.

As I kept going, I could see quite a lot of lights in the distance and as I came closer it became apparent that this was a major place. Douglas appeared on deck around 4:00am as we were coming ever closer to these lights, which I was pretty certain would be Scarborough. We approached the southern end of these lights and I could see some red and green navigation lights which I headed towards, as these would be an entrance.

As we came closer, it became even stranger and the buildings I saw appearing out of the night looked more like industrial buildings, not quite what I expected of Scarborough. I headed in real close and entered in between a set of navigation lights, but this took me into an enclosed area with a beach at the back, so I quickly turned around and made my way out of here, and had a look at the other side of this wooden pile pier.

At the other side, it appeared to be the entrance to a river, but as it was still dark, and the entrance was not at all clear, I opted to move further north to see what there was there. Heading north, there was even more industry and a little further along, what appeared to be a major river entrance. I was beginning to figure out in my mind that because I had stayed so far out overnight, that I must have missed Scarborough altogether, and this must be river Tees. There were no other rivers in this area.

There were some low lying islands to the north, and I decided to head west and cut inside them. As we sailed west, and as daylight came in, it became apparent, these were not islands, but an outcrop, and I would have to turn round and make my way out of the river channel I had inadvertently entered. By this time, daylight was well in, and I was pretty tired, having only slept two hours the previous night, so I decided I would have to go for a sleep, since Douglas and Johnny were now up.

I pointed out to Johnny were we were heading, and also pointed out the buoyed channel to him. I explained that this was for big ships, and we did not have to stay within the buoys, as long as we stayed fairly close to them. I then went below to have a much needed sleep. I was only down for around half an hour when Johnny called me and told me there was a problem. He said the tide was so strong that the boat would not steer the way he wanted it to. I climbed up on deck to find that we were well on the inside of the buoyed channel and we were aground.

There was a strong tide running, and I turned the boat this way and that, sometimes bumping along, sometimes getting nowhere. I had the guys move from one side of the boat to the other, forward to aft, and it seemed like we were getting nowhere. It would have been much easier if we had had the engine available to us, instead of just sails. In the end it took a full hour to get ourselves out of this potentially dangerous situation, and heading back out of the river again.

It was a lot farther than I thought to get out of this river and it was midday before we eventually rounded the final headland to get us back into the open sea. We started heading north again and were back on track, and I figured that Hartlepool would not be far away now. A little on our head, there were a couple of vessels working, and as we came nearer, one of them, a guard boat called us on VHF channel 16 and asked us to stay clear of the other vessel which was carrying out dredging for Easington refinery.

While I was talking to him, I asked if he could give me a distance to Hartlepool. He asked me to wait a minute and he would take a distance from his plotter. He called back within the minute and told me that it was ninety five miles to Hartlepool. I thought he must have misunderstood me and was giving me the distance to some other place, so I repeated my destination of Hartlepool and queried his answer. He confirmed his distance of ninety five miles. I looked at Johnny and Douglas, and I simply said "Where are we".

This had completely floored me and I could not understand what was going on. The first priority, I had to know where we were, so I went below and fired up the laptop, something which I should have done long before now. After a little searching, I discovered our location, just off Easington, which was on the north side of the Humber. My head was going a hundred miles per hour. That was the Humber we had just come out of, not the Tees. How did this happen? I just could not understand it, and had to think long and hard before I figured it out.

Firstly, when I looked at the compass, two nights previous and seen 310 degrees, it must have been 210 degrees. Because the compass was so dirty and unreadable, I had made a crucial error which cost us a whole day and much more hassle. Steering 210 degrees, I was heading down into the Wash, which was very shallow water everywhere, so this explained all the sand banks. The headland we had seen must have been the northwest corner of Norfolk around Hunstanton. When we turned around and headed north, the place with all the fireworks must have been the Butlins camp at Skegness or some similar place.

From this point, I had been heading in the right direction, but I was simply not where I thought I was and this is where all my confusion came from. Many things which had perplexed me over the past 30 hours now started to make sense. From thinking that we were near to Hartlepool, we were now faced with a 40 mile sail to the Scarborough which was the nearest suitable port for us heading north. There was never a thought about going back into the Humber to berth up in there, as we were just glad to be out of there.

I left Johnny and Douglas sailing north and went back to bed for a sleep again, as I was still very tired and after the excitement and adrenalin wore off, I was becoming very weary. I was down below for two hours again and when I got up, I could see the real Flamborough head in the distance, and was much happier with the progress. We had a meal in the early evening and after this, the wind started to die down, slowing our progress to around two miles per hour.

We decided that we would take turns through the night, and as it was fairly straight forward, the two guys should be OK on their own for a couple of hours each. We decided that we would set two hour watches from 10:00pm through to 4:00pm, giving us each four hours sleep during this period. I took the first watch, followed by Douglas, then lastly Johnny. As there was little wind, progress was pretty slow, but by the time my watch was over, we had well and truly rounded Flamborough head and could see clearly all along the Yorkshire coast, and I could point out to Douglas the lights I believed to be Scarborough and where he should head for.

Douglas was unfamiliar with the night vision and found it a little difficult to deal with the areas of light, and the absolutely pitch black parts in between. It appeared to him that there was something looming up in front of him, and he had to call me not long into his watch to be reassured that there were no obstacles in his way. Johnny had no problems and when he called me at 4:00am, we were very much closer to the lights which I believed to be Scarborough. As usual, when you think you are almost there, the last little bit seems to take for ever, and it was 6:00am before we finally sailed into port and could confirm that we were indeed in Scarborough.

It was not very easy getting in under sail, and we had to tie up in a temporary berth and get the assistance of the harbour master to move later. Once tied up, we quickly found a café above the fish market which opened early and served full English Breakfasts. We had a good tuck in before I went in search of an engineer to take a look at our engine. It had been almost three full days since we left Felixstowe, but we had packed a lot into those three days. It was good to be into port and tied up, and Johnny decided he would take his leave of us here, to ensure he made his appointment.

I found an engineer, but he said that he was very busy and would not manage to take a look at our engine that day. This was very disappointing, as it meant we were stuck in Scarborough until he could find the time to look at it and fix it. I found it strange that he was so busy that he was standing in his shop, still dressed in his good clothes, casually chatting with another guy as if he had all the time in the world. However, as he was the only engineer in the place, we had no option but to wait and enjoy this seaside resort.

It was a very busy place, and there were thousands of tourists around the harbour area. There were many boats taking tourists on a fifteen or thirty minute boat trip and they never stopped the entire day. One boat full of tourists stepped ashore and another bunch climbed on board. The second day we were there was a glorious sunny day, and the owners had to lay on an extra boat to cope with the demand.

It was a very good marina, but the facilities definitely let it down. An old building at the end of the pier, well away from the pontoon housed a very poor conversion to a shower and laundry area. The facilities were one of the poorest I had seen anywhere I have been up until now. Despite that, it was good to get a wash, and also to wash and freshen up my clothes.

On the Tuesday morning, the engineer appeared around 9:00am, which seemed to be first thing in the morning for him and after that entire wait, the engine was running in only 5 minutes. It was an airlock in the fuel pump which was causing the problem. Having been in Scarborough for over twenty four hours now, I was keen to get going and head north again, so having let the engine run for five minutes, I shut it down and went in search of the harbour master to pay my dues, so that we could head off.

Despite the poor facilities, Scarborough was probably the most expensive marina I had been in to date at around £23 for the night. I paid my bill and returned to the boat ready to go, only to find that the engine wouldn't start again, and the engineer was off to another project, and didn't seem to be much interested.

In the early afternoon Douglas and I took a walk up the road and I bought a few things. A nice new kettle for the stove; we had been using a pan up to now. I also bought a set of spanners which I needed for the engine and also a computer tablet which I would use for my charts from now on, the bigger screen much better than my small phone screen.

We returned to the boat and I tried to clear the airlock again, but didn't have much success. The engineer finally appeared around 5:00pm and again had the engine going in no time at all. It would appear that Jimmy Joiner hadn't taught me well enough and that I was not much more use around diesel engines than I was with petrol ones.

CHAPTER 16

Scarborough to Peterhead

Scarborough to Peterhead

With the engine now fixed, I did not waste any more time, but cast off and sailed from Scarborough around 6:00pm on the Tuesday evening. There was a fresh south westerly breeze and with the sails up, we were moving along nicely. I prepared myself for another all-night session and sent Douglas away to bed around 9:00pm. On the VHF, the coastguard was putting out an alert about a huge fifty feet tree which was floating in the Whitby area, so I was trying to keep my eyes peeled in the dark when I passed Whitby, as my little boat, only half of that size would not like to bump into the tree.

Once passed Whitby, there was a large bay perhaps twenty miles across around the Tees area, so I headed across that bay, well out from the land. The wind had also swung round to the North West and it was better to keep out from the land to get more wind in the sails, rather than too close a reach. I made pretty good progress all night and when Douglas appeared at around 6:00am, we were off Sunderland and still heading north.

As daylight came in, the wind dropped off and we were forced to start up the engine, rather than flop around at only one or two miles an hour. I left Douglas in charge and went below for a much needed sleep. Two hours later I was back up to find ourselves crossing the Tyne and heading north at a fine rate.

It was a pleasant enough day and we continued to plod north around the main headlands until we came to our chosen nightly destination of Amble, a river port protected by a sizable island at the entrance and a rocky foreshore. We were approaching Amble through this channel when the engine picked the worst time to splutter and die.

I used one of our spare tanks to quickly top up the fuel tank, but the engine still would not start. On inspection, there was fuel coming out of a loose bleed screw on top of the oil pump, so I guess that is why the engine died, having pumped all our fuel into the bilges. I tried a number of times, in vain to bleed the pump and get the engine going, but in the end had to sail into Amble under the very light winds there were.

If nothing else, I was truly becoming an expert at entering into ports under only sail power. Unfortunately, by the time we had managed to get berthed up, again aided by a local fisherman, the local firm of engineers had already finished for the day, so we would have to wait until morning to have the engine looked at. I did try again a few times myself, but still could not get it going.

Amble was a very nice marina though. There were plenty of berths and fantastic facilities. We both had a shower and a change of clothes and then headed up the road in search of eating places. We found a small pub which advertised traditional food, although we had to walk quite a bit to get it. We had a main course, but weren't overly impressed with it, and I actually topped it up at a chip shop which we found later on, down near the harbour, which we would have been better to go to at first, if we had only turned the right direction when we exited the marina.

We bedded down early that night and I caught up with my sleep. There was no hurry in the morning as we had to wait for the engineer again to come and look at the engine. While we were waiting, we got all our fuel tanks topped up, as we were lying at the fuel berth anyway, so we would be ready to go once the engine was fixed. The engineer appeared just after 9:00am and after his customary five minutes; we were once again ready to go. Again it was an airlock and I began to wonder why I couldn't manage to get that fixed with my nice new shiny spanners.

We left Amble at 10:00am and headed north again. It was a glorious day, but unfortunately there was not a breath of wind and we had to motor all the way to Peterhead. We left Amble and headed north towards the Farne Islands. As we would be cutting across the huge bight formed by the two mighty Scottish rivers of the Tay and Forth, I decided that we would just stay on the outside of all these islands and head north away from the coastline which was now starting to head in a north westerly direction.

All that day, we edged further away from the land until it was only a distant smudge on the western horizon. As night fell, I could begin to see some lights and watched as lights from the north slowly appeared as we started to come back towards the Scottish coastline again. The very first light I could see, from a long, long way away was the top of the TV mast at Durris, south west of Aberdeen. Slowly other lights appeared and by the time Douglas came on deck at 6:00am, were off Portlethen, on the south side of Aberdeen.

I needed to get a few hours' sleep again, so I left Douglas at the helm and warned him to be very vigilant crossing Aberdeen bay as the area was littered with oil related vessels which anchored up there awaiting their next job, rather than pay expensive harbour dues. All went well though and when I got up a couple of hours later, we were approaching the Ythan estuary, and were well on our way to Peterhead.

We finally docked in Peterhead marina around midday on the Friday and I decided that we would leave the boat there and go home, as while I had been away, Pearl's mum had landed in the hospital and was quite ill. Moira, pearl's sister made some "mince and tatties" for us and after a fine feed, Paul, my nephew gave us a run home to Gamrie, ending a nine day very eventful trip.

CHAPTER 17

Winter's work

Winter's work

As I knew when I bought the boat, I would have a whole lot of work to do over the winter, and at this moment, in early October, I am still trying to throw it all around in my head and figure out what gets done first.

I am fairly happy with the outside hull of the boat. It is not very tidy, but I think I can leave that until next year, take the boat ashore and do a proper job of scraping the hull back to the bare boat and have it finished properly. I just wouldn't have time for that this year, so it is best left until next winter.

I do have a number of outside jobs though and I did start the tidying up at the end of September. I took down all the running rigging which was very grubby and took them all home to wash and evaluate if they are Ok or will need replaced. I don't think the boat has been used a lot and the problem is more filth that wear. The sails are the same. I haven't pulled them all out of their bags yet, but at a quick glance I wonder if some of them have ever actually been used, although again they need a good clean up.

I want to fit roller reefing to the head sail as going forward to hank on is not very good when you are single handed. I would also like to fit dodgers, a spray hood and sail cover/stack pack. I have located a business online which makes dodgers and spray hood kits at very reasonable prices, so I will most likely avail myself of these services. They will also provide me with the materials I need to make my own stack pack and lazy jack system. Hopefully Pearl will help me out with this one as she is much better at this than me.

I bought some polish and started by polishing one side of the hull which did bring it up much better. Next trip home at the end of October, hopefully I can get the other side done and also the topsides. All the wood on the boat will need to be taken off, sanded down and varnished, as it doesn't look like it has been done in the past ten years.

I also want to fit a tiller pilot, which will steer the boat rather than me always having to stay at the helm. This will be invaluable to me as it will allow me to go below, make food and check my charts and progress while we are underway. At the moment, if I am single handed, which I would be most of the time, I cannot leave the tiller for 5 seconds, and the boat would be off in another direction.

On the inside, I have a few essential jobs, but most are just for my comfort. This boat was designed to have a sealed cabin compartment, but someone saw fit to drill a hole in the floor of the cabin, and the contents of the bilge have come up and made a terrible diesel smell which has gone through the entire boat. I have now blocked up this hole, but I think there are other areas which the seal of the cabin needs to be checked and confirmed.

The upholstery was particularly stinking, and when I got them home to my garage, I wasted no time in cutting the cloth off and putting it in the skip. I will have to try and clean up and de-stink the foam before recovering it ready for the new season. I want to shelf off the forward cabin for storage space, as I will never use that for sleeping in. At the moment the boat has seven berths if you count the forward cabin, but I will reduce that to four or even three berths.

The biggest change inside, and I am still not sure if I will proceed with it, is that I would like to dispense with the quarter berth on the starboard side and make it into a locker accessed from the cockpit. This would give me much more locker space on deck and I would lose a space inside which isn't much use anyway. This would also allow me to fit a fixed proper galley rather than a slide away one.

The other major tasks I have in mind is a complete rewire of the boat and an overhaul of my engine. As you have seen, engines are not my department, so I will contract that out to an expert, but I hope that I will be able to rewire the boat myself.

All in all, it is a fair winter's work list, so if you have any spare time, feel free to offer.

PART 4

A look ahead to Sail with Jim 2013

Part Four – A look ahead to Sail with Jim 2013

I have secured a permanent berth in Peterhead and at the moment, I think I will take the boat home here each winter to allow me to get my winter work done, but I have also secured a summer moorings in Broadford bay, in Skye. This should be a better base than Oban, as I can get a train from Keith right to Kyle, with only the one change at Inverness. Once off the train at Kyle, a bus will run through all the villages in Skye and will be timed to match the train arrivals.

I am planning at the moment to take the boat round there in April. The exact timing will depend on my work schedule and time off. The route I will take will depend on the weather. If it is decent weather, I will go across to Wick, through the Pentland Firth and round Cape Wrath, but if the weather is in any way dodgy, I will go through the canal and up through the sound of Mull as I did this year.

Once the boat is round there, I will use Broadford as a base to do some cruising on the west coast of Scotland with my most cherished desire being for a trip to St Kilda and the Flannan Isles. There are a number of other destinations knocking about in this crazy head including Northern Ireland, the western isles and many of the small islands between Skye and the Clyde.

There are many places you can sail and cruise on the west coast, and I hope to have much more exciting adventures to tell you about in my second book which should be out around this time next year. If you would like to be part of that adventure, even just for a few days sailing, get in touch with me. I am always happy to have company. I don't like sailing alone, but have to out of necessity.

Of course, I am only talking about 2013 here. Beyond that who knows where I will end up?

PART 5

Update 2021

2021

Well, you have heard the oft-quoted words of Robbie Burns, "*The best laid schemes o' Mice an' Men Gang aft agley*". That was certainly true for me. I had a fantastic year in 2013 but never quite managed the opportunity to fulfil my dream of a trip out to the St Kilda group of Islands. I had a late start in 2014 due to engine trouble, but I eventually put an outboard on the boat and left Peterhead in June. Despite the late start, I had a great summer and visited places as far apart as Stornoway and the Crinan canal. I even went through the infamous Corryvreken channel.

At the end of that year, I had the boat taken ashore in a small boatyard just south of Oban rather than sail her home. I got her painted and re-engined and ready for the 2015 season. That is when my whole world changed. In January 2015, my marriage of 33 years came to an end, and it was a pretty lousy year for me. I lost heart in the boat and ended up selling her for less than half of what I had paid for her.

It took a year to sort myself out, then I met Janice, who is now my new wife. I also picked up a job down in the Congo, West Africa, and we moved to live in Tenerife, where I had the old longing come back. I had to scratch the itch and chartered a 39-foot yacht for a week out of

Las Galletas. There were undoubtedly a few more good stories that week, but that is for another time. Safe to say, the Canaries, with WAZ (Wind acceleration zones), is a whole different ball game from the west coast of Scotland. It's not for the faint-hearted and certainly wasn't for Janice.

That old itch is still there, and once I get settled back into the UK and get roots down, I think I will start scanning the for sale pages again.

This marks the end of the book. If you have enjoyed this book, we would ask you to help us.

1. We would be grateful if you could leave a review of the book on Amazon or other place you bought it. These reviews are the lifeblood of my business, and without them, I would have no new customers, and I could no longer write books.
2. I would welcome you to contact us through my author website at www.jamesgwhitelaw.com. I can assure you and I am a real person and do not use a pen name. I will answer any questions you have as soon as I am able.
3. Finally, let your friends know that you read my book and enjoyed it on your social media pages.

Thanks for reading the book.

www.ingramcontent.com/pod-product-compliance
Lightning Source LLC
Chambersburg PA
CBHW021155080526
44588CB00008B/356